# Praise for Volumes 1 and 2

McKenna—using down-to-earth ences to deliver a message expressing spirit of the Good News—knows the value of prayer, or vigilance in virtue and the supreme importance of charity for the homeless, the derelict. These homilies in print will continue to inspire a wider reading public.
— Father James Gray, O.S.B., *The Prairie Messenger*, Canadian publication

What impressed me most was the spirit of his sermons. [McKenna] says more in three minutes than most homilies manage to say in a half-hour. And it's something you can take with you.
— Steve Culen, Retired Executive Director, A.F.S.C.M.E./Illinois

I think [McKenna's two volumes] are excellent. . . . They are easily "digestible," interesting, and will bring peace and wisdom to readers. They are also the sort of books you could give away to anyone re-gardless of religious denomination, with appeal to a large range of age groups.
— Colleen McGuiness-Howard, *The Record*, Western Australian newspaper

Father tells [his] congregation, 'I'll only speak for three minutes,' and he means it! He has a stop-watch at the pulpit. His homilies are . . . challenging and inspirational.
— Reverend John M. (Hop-a-long) Cassidy, Assoc. Pastor, St. Daniel the Prophet Church

These are real masterpieces which should be savored quietly, when the soul needs something special—a boost, a restraining touch, a quiet smile, an insight into some puzzling truth or even a Kleenex® for the occasional tear. . . . He writes of these spiritual treasures with a child-like simplicity that is wonderful to share.
— Father Thomas C. Donlan, O.P., *Homiletic & Pastoral Review*, national U.S. publication

Every week, McKenna prints his homilies in a bulletin for passersby – and later compiles them in book form to inspire God-fearing individuals far beyond the airport walls. Hopefully, the inspirational books will keep coming.

—Rena Fulka, *The Star* newspaper

Short and sweet. That's what I like.

—anonymous police officer stationed at Chicago's Midway Airport after Mass

# I'll Only Speak for 3 Minutes

VOLUME 3

# I'LL ONLY SPEAK FOR 3 MINUTES

## VOLUME 3

## The Personal Best of Chicago's Midway Airport Chaplain

FATHER GEORGE MCKENNA

VCA PUBLISHING
Honolulu • Los Angeles • Chicago

I'll Only Speak for 3 Minutes, Volume 3
The Personal Best of Chicago's Midway Airport Chaplain
VCA Publishing / October 2000

Copyright ©2000 by Vedic Cultural Association/George McKenna

Book design by Symes Production & Design
Design concept by Joseph P. Higgins

Cover Photo by Carrie Leubben

Printed in the United States of America

ISBN 1-928869-08-4

To all
Benefactors
of the
Chicago Midway Airport Chapel,
large and small,
their generosity and support
make possible
the benevolent intentions
of its charitable mission.

# Contents

# Introduction

I am very pleased to present Volume Three of Father McKenna's world-famous homilies. The sermons in this edition were personally selected by Father as his favorite parables. He chose them from over 500 unpublished homilies given in the past twelve years at the Midway Airport Chapel.

I first met Father McKenna while attending Quigley Preparatory Seminary South in the late 1960s. All the seminarians loved Father for his kindness, humility and wisdom. Twenty-five years and many, many travels later, I began visiting Chicago frequently, while working on a book about my life as an astrologer to billionairess Doris Duke. I would often attend Mass at the airport chapel with my mother, Marie. There I met Father McKenna once again.

One day, as Father started his homily with the words, "I'll only speak for three minutes," I had a flash of divine inspiration. "That's a book," I exclaimed to myself. I mentioned this to my family. They all loved the idea. We then approached Father, who enthusiastically embraced the concept. In fact, he had always wanted to publish but had no idea how to go about it. I assured him that VCA Publishing could do it.

I assembled a competent crew to design and produce the book. In September 1998, after six months of working feverishly, the first volume of *I'll Only Speak for 3*

*Minutes* was finally available. We had done it. The books sold like hotcakes. People were buying multiple copies and giving them to friends and relatives. The Mayor got a copy. The Cardinal received a copy. Rave reviews came in from across the country. By January 1999, we were almost out of books and needed to reprint. Based upon such favorable response, we produced a second volume, which was released in April the same year. By that time, Father's first book was receiving praise and testimonials from all over the world.

On July 10, just before his 80th birthday, Erin O'Donnell, Deputy Commissioner of Aviation at Midway Airport, presented Father McKenna with a framed letter from Chicago Mayor Richard M. Daley in recognition of his years of service at the municipal airport.

What follows is the amazing story of how Father started the chapel at Midway Airport, and, of course, thirty-seven of his favorite, famous, three-minute homilies. Enjoy yourself and God bless.

—James E. Higgins III

### The Inside Story of Midway Chapel

One cold January day, while sitting in the terminal at Midway Airport, I said to myself, "Wouldn't it be a good thing if religious services could be held somewhere here." It was 1987, and not one religious service had been held at the airport since its opening in 1927.

I put this possibility before Padre Pio, whom I had

admired from the early days of my priesthood. A Capuchin monk in Italy, he had inspired so many people with his strong faith in the Mass and the Eucharist. In the history of the Catholic Church, Padre Pio has been the only priest bearing the stigmata of all five wounds of Christ.

A year before Midway Chapel was to open, I found myself at the Foyer Sacerdotal, a house for priests in Paris, France. Come dinner time, one French priest came and sat next to me—and did for the following three evenings.

On the third night, an American priest asked this French clergyman for me what kind of work he did. His answer stunned me: "I am Father Andre. I am in charge of promoting the cause of Padre Pio for Sainthood in all of France."

Father Andre went on to tell me, through my fellow American interpreter, that he had known Padre Pio well and had gone regularly for confession to this holy man. From his station wagon, this French reverend gave me many photos of the stigmatic priest, who had died in 1968. I vowed to Padre Pio that we would always have his photo in our airport if he brought about its opening. The Chapel has kept that promise.

Pope John Paul II beatified Padre Pio in Rome on May 2, 1999. The next step will be canonization of the humble Capuchin monk. We continue to pray to Padre Pio for help at the Midway Airport Chapel.

During 1987 and the first months of 1988, the people

of Our Lady of the Snows Church, located near the airport, prayed for the opening of the new chapel. As an associate pastor in the parish, I had shared my dream with them.

At the same time, I visited a friend dying of cancer, Bill Sikon. As we sat together, he wrote on a piece of paper: "Chapel – how does it look?" I said to Bill, "When you get to Heaven in a few days, you will have to pray for us." He died within the week.

A few days later, a major breakthrough took place, where before there had been no hope. Was Bill working for us in Heaven? His interest in the chapel amazed me; with death at his elbow, Bill was concerned about its future.

Mr. Bill Krystiniak, then Alderman of our airport ward, stepped forward to become a key person in dealing with the Department of Aviation for the City of Chicago. Without him, we would have made little progress in convincing others of the worthiness of a chapel in the airport.

I believe Padre Pio inspired both these Bills to become such devoted friends of the chapel.

Even when the late Cardinal Bernadin and city officials gave their permission for religious services to be held in Midway Airport, no one could find space for the chapel. Was our dream of a place of worship to stop at this – after eighteen months of effort and prayer? People in Our Lady of the Snows were offering their pains and sicknesses to God for its opening. We thank all these unknown saints for their unselfish help.

Suddenly, Midway Airlines, under the direction of David Hinson, came up with a most generous offer. Midway Airlines, to its great credit, allowed us the use of one of its gates on Saturday evenings and Sunday mornings. All Midway Airlines employees – as well as all the airport workers and people of other airlines – have shown the chapel workers a courtesy and a spirit of helpfulness far beyond the call of duty.

We have prayed for the success of the airlines and the good health of their employees and all other airport workers at every Mass offered during these last twelve years at Midway.

At the first Mass ever celebrated in Midway Airport – Saturday, July 24, 1988 – a young woman guitarist, Miss Erin Solkowski from Our Lady of the Snows Parish, accompanied the overflowing congregation in song. This was her only visit to the airport chapel. No one else has ever played a musical instrument in celebration of our Masses.

A few weeks later, Erin's mother told me an amazing story. Erin's middle name is Pio. Ann Solkowski needed help at the birth of Erin and prayed to Padre Pio, promising that she would name the child – boy or girl – Pio. Erin was delivered safely. Padre Pio was saying at that first Mass in the airport, "See, I am with you." Thank you, Padre Pio.

In October of 1998, we celebrated the 10ᵗʰ Anniversary Mass and the publication of Volume One. Over 150 people attended this special event – the largest of any chapel congregation since its founding.

Erin, now married, returned. Once again, music from her guitar and the sound of her lovely voice praised God, this time in concert with her sister Fiona, who is also a talented singer. We have had no other musical accompaniment at the chapel in the past dozen years. Thank you, Erin and Fiona.

Another Erin, Ms. O'Donnell, Deputy Commissioner of Aviation at Midway Airport, has done much to find a fixed location for our little house of worship. Through her continuing efforts and those of many others, the Airport Chapel should be in its permanent quarters, situated in the new terminal building, presently under construction, by the end of the year 2001.

—Father George McKenna

## Midway Airport Acknowledgments

In addition to Padre Pio, Bill Sikon, Bill Krystiniak, the late Joseph Cardinal Bernadin, and David Hinson, I would also like to thank and acknowledge others who were instrumental in starting Midway Airport Chapel: Congressman William Lipinski; former Midway Airport Manager, Richard DiPietro; Mayor Richard M. Daley; Richard Guzior; Gene Zell of Zell Printing; Joe Waddell (R.I.P.); Reverend Daniel Holihan; Everett G. Rand;

Erin O'Donnell; Al Perez; Matt Marich; and the Midway Chapel Volunteer Workers.

## Book Acknowledgments

I am indebted to Southwest Airlines, whose employees, in coordination with Captain Jack Huffman, Susanne Griffith, Marie Higgins, and the Aumann Family, transported two shipments of books from Nashville to Chicago free of charge.

My sincere appreciation goes to the men and women who helped promote Volumes 1 and 2 in their respective parishes, religious groups and social organizations.

To my publishers, James and Joseph Higgins, their ceaseless efforts in bringing my literary dreams to fruition have not gone unnoticed.

For all my family and friends, too numerous to name, who spread the word—you have my many thanks and prayers.

# The Wisest Choice Of All

A short time ago, a man approached me after our Saturday evening Mass in Midway Airport. Some 20 years ago, he was a parishioner in a parish where I was pastor. He refreshed my mind about a homily I had given. "One day you said in a homily, 'Sometimes I am so busy in a day that I don't have a chance to give much time to prayer. On such a day, I fill in the little spaces of time with short prayers, my favorite one being, *Jesus of Nazareth*.'" My former parishioner went on to say, "I have said that prayer every day since I heard you."

What a wise choice my friend made! I probably thought on that morning 20 years ago, "another homily falling on deaf ears." But, no, this man decided that speaking with the Lord every day was a wonderful idea. He began to make prayer as much a part of his daily life as his breathing. When I say, 'Jesus of Nazareth,' I know the demons fear the name of Jesus, the Lord. 'Nazareth' reminds me of the earthly life Jesus led with all His loving ways of living. Still, in 1999, that prayer falls frequently off my lips.

Ask me, a priest of 55 years, "What helped you the

most in staying in the priesthood?" I would answer, "Daily prayer!" Through prayer, I brought the power of God, the Father, the Son and the Holy Spirit into my life. I say daily because the challenges to despair, to deserting God, come every hour of the day. This was the wisest decision I have ever made.

A month ago, a woman spoke to me after a Sunday morning Mass in the airport. She said, "Fifty-five years ago I remember when you told us how to remember to say our morning prayers. You said, 'At evening time, put your shoes underneath your bed. In the morning, when you get up, you have to go on your knees to get your shoes. This will remind you to pray.'" Evidently, she had been using this method for prayer, otherwise she would have forgotten my words. These are true stories!

*... the challenges to despair, to deserting God, come every hour of the day.*

Yes, the wisest thing we can do is to share our life with an All-Loving God. Some look upon prayer as burdensome, something easily put off. How short-sighted! When we do not pray, God does not remove Himself from us. We move away from God. Prayer brings adventure into our life with possibilities unlimited for growth in Christ-like ways of living.

# The Priest Is God's Almoner

In the Middle Ages, kings lived in great castles with high walls and protective moats, water-filled ditches. In his household, the king appointed one man, his "almoner," to dispense his charities to the poor in the district. In much the same way, a priest acts as God's almoner, offering the riches of God's mercy to the needy. Yes, I, as a priest, can dispense His mercy and forgiveness to all seeking peace with God.

Because God is an Ocean of Mercy, I can give generous portions to His poor. God gives me an inexhaustible supply! No sin is so great that I can't forgive. The Parable of the Prodigal Son tells of the love a father has for his wayward son. Through this story, Jesus told us of His Heavenly Father's love for each one of us.

Do we know of anyone in our family circle or among our friends or co-workers who is away from God? Perhaps this person might fear to approach God's human agent, the priest, for forgiveness. This is understandable! In a wrong way of thinking, the man/woman might have decided that confession of sins for a 40-year period would be too difficult to make. Maybe the reader, away from confession for many years, is thinking this, too: "impossible to determine number of sins," "priest will scold me," or "too embarrassing."

Now is the time to approach God's almoner for a soul-cleansing confession. Being a sinner myself, I welcome with open arms all people away from God. It makes no difference whether the person has been away from confession for forty years or one year. I can bring God's peace to the person's soul in a minute or two.

*... a priest acts as God's almoner, offering the riches of God's mercy to the needy.*

I never ask questions (or rarely so). Nor do I judge or criticize anyone! Numbers are not necessary for sins. Before coming to confession, the penitent goes over the Ten Commandments and determines an estimation of his/her offenses against them. The penitent need not go into details, just a general declaration is sufficient. I discourage details. In this way, one can make a ten- or fifty-year confession in a minute, indeed, a very sincere one in this short time.

The longer a person is away from confession, the more delighted I am to be of service. What a compliment to me that this man or woman trusts me to offer His forgiveness to the penitent and bring the person's soul to perfect condition, the way it was at Baptism. God gives me tremendous powers for this.

# You Shall Never Hunger
# Or Thirst Again

The shelves of the local supermarkets hold all sorts of food and drinks to satisfy the physical hungers and thirsts of their customers. However, these giant food stores cannot satisfy the spiritual hungers and thirsts of their patrons. One day, Jesus spoke these awesome words, "No one who comes to Me shall ever be hungry. No one who believes in Me shall ever thirst."

With these words, Jesus promised amazing things in helping us understand the mysteries of life. Oftentimes, in years past, in quiet corners of splendid Gothic churches of Paris, I have come upon young people, sitting on the floor, praying in quiet, subdued song before an image of Christ or Mary. Usually, a few guitarists led them in barely audible harmony of chants of praise.

These young people had learned this practice of quiet prayer at Taize, the famous ecumenical monastery, about 150 miles south of Paris. The monastery at Taize, an isolated place, under the guidance of

Brother Roger, a holy man about my age, attracts young people from all over the world.

The youngsters come to Taize to find meaning in life, to seek a deeper friendship with Christ, to heal the wounds of their minds and hearts. As St. Matthew said some eighty times in his Gospel, "Jesus is Lord!" So the youthful pilgrims make this the theme of their stay at Taize. Visiting there changed my life.

All believers in Jesus can imitate the youngsters of Paris and Taize. Like the young people in the churches of Paris, one can draw aside to a quiet place in the home, away from the noise of family life. One could sit on cushions or pillows, something I do, before an image of Christ or Mary.

*The youngsters come to Taize to find meaning in life, to seek a deeper friendship with Christ.*

The believer can speak from the heart in words of friendship with Christ, reminding Him of His promises mentioned above. "I want a deeper friendship with You. Help me to see the meaning of life. My weaknesses dismay me. My grief is like a heavy stone in my heart."

Jesus never made empty promises. Quietly keep whispering to Him, "Jesus is Lord." My experience at Taize has left an indelible mark on my spirit. It opened a new door in my heart to what could happen in my life.

# Am I Spending Too Much Time
# On Red Barns?

The following story made a lasting impression on me. It helped me look into my life to search out ways of making it more fruitful. An art teacher gave one of his students an assignment to paint the sunset of that particular day. Some time later, toward the end of the day, the teacher found his student painting the shingles on the roof of a red barn. All the while, the sun was sinking faster and faster in the west. The exasperated teacher said, "Why are you spending so much time on the barn? The sunset is your main concern!"

God has given us a commission to paint a masterpiece of our own life with a time limit attached. Perhaps we are spending too much energy on things like the red barn, not related to the main task. Life is quickly disappearing while we give too much time to trivia.

A while ago, I bought a thought-provoking book downtown, *Don't Sweat the Small Stuff, and It's All Small Stuff.* The author touches on many happenings in life where we could be wasting our time and energy. Call them the *red barns*! All the while we are missing out on the grand scenario of life.

Be conscious of what is happening in our life. Consider the following. We are cut off in traffic. Instead of boiling over with anger, a real waste of energy, let the driver have his way. Pity him for his great hurry. We keep our sense of well-being. If things are not perfect in home, work or society in general, accept the situation as it is. Refuse to be a reformer of the world.

*God has given us a commission to paint a masterpiece of our own life with a time limit attached.*

Believe that gentle, relaxed people can still be super-achievers.

Be aware of how negative thinking can snowball. The more time and energy we give to what is troubling us, the worse we feel. Refer this to fears, worries and anxieties. Cut off these ideas trying to take over. It works for me.

Before going to work, school or housework, take time out, even 30 seconds, and ask yourself, "How am I going to live this day?" In my own personal life, I found this effective in beginning the day with some goals in mind. I'm not going to give a lot of time to *red barns* today, while missing out on the central theme, making my life a masterpiece of God. A simple goal I often choose is: "Lord, help me to be a loving person today."

# Faith Lights Up The Glory Road

S ome years ago, I had an unusual experience in the Holy City of Jerusalem. The Old City rests on the side of a mountain, with the result that all the streets go up or down, with no level ones. One morning, on coming out of the Franciscan Hospice, my residence, about 5:00 am, I planned to walk to the Church of the Holy Sepulcher. I was to offer Mass on Mt. Calvary in this ancient shrine built by St. Helena around the year 300 AD.

I stepped out into complete darkness. Heavy clouds covered the moon. The street lights were turned off. I couldn't see my hands in front of me. Since I had often walked this downhill street, about a block long with its seven turns, I started off to the church. The narrow road, about 30 feet wide, had walls rising up at both sides. I kept my hand on the side wall as I cautiously put my foot ahead of me to catch the beginning of the next step. I made it safely through the seven turns, although the last step almost did me in— a fearful journey.

The next morning, the same conditions prevailed. This time I had a small pencil-shaped flashlight. Its little beam of light aimed at my feet brought me quickly to Holy Sepulcher Church. What a difference the light made! I couldn't see down the street. I just had enough light to take the next step!

We can compare this walk above to our daily journey in life. The light is the gift of Faith we receive in Baptism. As we experience the darkness of our walk on the Glory Road, faith in God helps us to avoid injuries, dangerous spills and despair. Faith lights up the twists and turns. We believe in the Presence of the Lord, His Constant Love abiding with us. With no Faith, people move along in hellish darkness, exposed to all kinds of miseries.

*As we experience the darkness of our walk on the Glory Road, faith in God helps us to avoid injuries, dangerous spills and despair.*

Sometimes, this walk takes me to my personal Hill of Calvary. There I am nailed to my own cross of suffering. By the light of my Faith, I believe Jesus promises to support me, to be at my side, at times carrying me on His Back. Jesus did not promise to shield us from these painful experiences. The Glory Road is unmapped, at times bringing us to places we never expected to go! At times, everything there will not be wonderful!

Pity the people without Faith! The Pharisees were

blind to Christ's Love. They did not walk as children of light. Indeed, they rejected Christ, the Light of the World, thus sealing their self-destruction. Faith is believing that the Lord is in Sovereign Control, that He will never desert us in our pain.

One pastor prayed for a good position in some growing church, where people would like him and his family. His Glory Road led him to "Smokey Mountain," a garbage dump outside a big city in the Philippine Islands. He and his children scavenge for food, along with 20,000 others. Christ is there with him! So he delights in it!

*Landscape just outside Old City of Jerusalem.*

# A 1997 Pilgrimage In Jerusalem

Tuesday, January 7, 1997, Jerusalem. This morning our little group of three go five miles south of Jerusalem to Shepherds' Fields. In this historic place, on the first Christmas night, the angel announced the "good news" of the Birth of the Messiah in nearby Bethlehem to the shepherds watching over their flocks. Just the three of us stand at the altar in this small chapel, really a cave carved out of rock, as we begin Mass with the hymn, *Silent Night, Holy Night.*

We celebrate the Midnight Mass of Christmastime with the Scriptures telling of the angels' visit to this lonely hillside. At this message of the angels, the history of the world took a hundred degree turn for the better. "Today, there is born to you a Savior in Bethlehem. You will find Him wrapped in swaddling clothes." My two friends, Captain Jack, a Southwest Airlines pilot, and Tom, an Albuquerque, New Mexico lawyer, and I finish Mass with the hymn, *O Come, All Ye Faithful.* After Mass, I thank God for the gift of faith enabling me to treasure the Messiah, born in nearby Bethlehem 2000 years ago. This was my first Mass in Shepherds' Fields. This being the Octave week of the

Feast of the Epiphany, we three pilgrims, like the Three Kings, go to Bethlehem to the Grotto of the Nativity to offer our Gifts to the Holy Child—our love, loyalty and friendship.

Wednesday, January 8, 1997. The Garden of Gethsemane lies just outside the walls of the Old City to the east, at the foot of the Mount of Olives. Next to the Garden stands the Church of All Nations (so called because people from across the world contributed to its construction in 1930). A 20-minute walk downhill from our residence brings Tom and me to this Place of Great Sadness.

Not only Judas betrayed the Master in this Garden, but also the other disciples showed cowardice. With a few pithy words, the Gospels say, "They stood at a distance."

*Some weeks later, in February 1997, I came face to face with a stretch of days of physical pain and the Lord's words came often to my lips.*

In all my past visits to Gethsemane, the weaknesses of the disciples of Christ reminded me of my own frailty and the ever-present possibility of my choosing creatures over the Master. At our 9:00 am Mass, I plead with the Lord to take me in death rather than be His betrayer by sin.

Afterwards, sitting in the darkness of the church, I think of the words Christ spoke in His Agony, "Father, if it be possible, let this cup of suffering pass, but not My Will but Thine be done." Some weeks later, in February 1997, I came face to face with a stretch of days of physical pain and the Lord's words came often to my lips.

Saturday, January 11, 1997. Mass at the Sixth Station. On this warm, sunny day, I enter the cave-like chapel at the Sixth Station to offer Mass. Here Veronica lived in the time of Christ. As He passed by her home on the way to Calvary, she courageously wiped His bloody Face with a towel. I find the Mass a wonderful, peaceful experience! After Mass, Tom, my fellow pilgrim, had much discomfort with a running nose, with no handkerchief or paper tissue handy. Much like Veronica, I gave him a clean, unused hanky to ease his condition.

*Church of All Nations, Garden of Gethesame.*

# The Best Kept Secret
# On The Glory Road

I love St. Joseph, "The Quiet Man" of the Gospels! Although only mentioned four times in the Gospels, this gentle, prayerful man found himself in trouble each time. The woman he was to marry evidently was carrying a child. Only an angel calmed his troubled heart. At Bethlehem, Joseph settled for a drafty stable for the birth of the Holy Child, while shortly after the birth, an angel's message took him and his family into dark, mysterious Egypt. A desperate Joseph sought the lost Boy Jesus at age 12!

No wonder the Church, through the centuries, has cried out to all in trouble, *Ite Ad Joseph,* "Go To Joseph!" After Ordination in 1944, I was assigned to a school for dependent children, Maryville, with an enrollment of 850 boys and girls. Every night, after a 15-hour day, I came to the school chapel and knelt before Joseph's altar. Above his statue were inscribed the words, *Ite Ad Joseph.* I prayed, "Dear St. Joseph, you had only One Foster Child, but I am foster father to 800 children. You must help me to be the kind of foster father you were—kind, patient, prayerful."

Without doubt, Joseph heard my prayers in the dark silence of the late nights. I mean to say, after doing my tour of duty for five years, I went on to other work almost a normal person. Night after night, this good friend gave me determination to continue to care for God's little ones, my foster children.

I would like to shout out to the world what a powerful intercessor we have in the Foster Father of Jesus and the Husband of Mary! Consider him the Best Kept Secret on the Glory Road! All through the years after Maryville, I continued to call on my dear friend, Joseph, for all my needs in the priesthood. Because I pray with absolute faith in his care for me, he answers my prayers in a sometimes miraculous way—especially in my travels. Tell everyone what a big difference Joseph can make in our efforts to lead a holy life! We don't want him to languish in the shadows, thereby robbing ourselves of his powerful and loving presence in our lives!

*Dear St. Joseph, you had only One Foster Child, but I am foster father to 800 children.*

If we find ourselves in a pit of despondency in an addiction to something displeasing to God, beg Joseph the carpenter to build a ladder so that we can climb out of it. In Alaska, in my time with the Eskimos, every day I walked up and down in our little

Mission Chapel, always stopping at its back to put my hands on the feet of the life-sized statue of Joseph. It was my way of saying, "Joseph, I trust in your help!" I love Joseph!

# Conquer The Demons!

M y good friend and golfing companion, Father John Nicola, ranks as a top expert in the USA in the field of demons and their presence in the world. From the time he wrote his doctrinal thesis on demons back in 1955 in the seminary until now, Father John has immersed himself in the study of evil spirits. A Chicago priest, he served as consultant for the well-known and, at times, terrifying movie, "The Exorcist." In the movie, a priest, through prayers and holy water, commands the evil spirits to leave a young girl. For many years my friend has lectured on university campuses across our country. He truly believes in the presence of demons.

What is the most powerful prayer to say as the demons approach to take us from God? The Jesus Prayer is simply a few words spoken to God with the Holy Name of Jesus included. The Prayer has come to us from the Russian Church of the 11th century. There is no Name on earth so Powerful and Holy as His Name. What I like about this Prayer is that it can be said quickly. "Jesus, protect me." It's impossible to be distracted while saying it.

By using His Name in times of stress or temptations from the devils, I bring the Holy One, Jesus, into my heart. At the mention of His Name, the devils shudder in fear. Suppose that we are being tempted to break God's wishes for us! We can sense the evil swirling about ourselves. We are conscious of our own weakness. At such a time, in microseconds, we can bring the Name of Jesus to our lips. "Jesus, do not leave me. Stay with me."

The story goes that, one day, the devils gathered in their recreation room to discuss the strategy of winning people over to their side. They finally agreed that the best method was to make people believe that there are no evil spirits. "This will catch people off guard." I once printed one of these bulletins with the evil happenings of one day in the USA, such as one suicide every two minutes, a murder every three minutes and so through a long list of offenses against God. No devils around?

*By using His Name, in times of stress or temptations from the devils, I bring the Holy One, Jesus, into my heart.*

This Jesus Prayer brings the Power of the Lord into my being—His Strength, His Mercy, His Love, His Goodness. I am not left alone in these present difficult circumstances. My shaking knees receive support. I feel a new surge of life in my inner self! Prayer can take place anywhere, not just when I am in Church or on my knees. No! When I am walking, working, washing dishes, driving, these words of the Jesus Prayer can come to my lips to enliven me against any onslaughts of the demonic spirits. Have a supply of Holy Water in your home. Sprinkle often!

# Jerusalem 1997

On a cold New Year's Day, 1997, along with two traveling companions, I took off from O'Hare Airport for Tel Aviv, Israel. The El Al (Israeli Airlines) 747 stopped at Montreal and filled all empty seats with passengers. After an in-air flight of 12 hours, we landed safely on Thursday, January 2, at the Ben Gurion Airport in the early afternoon. A 45-minute ride in a van brought us up the steep expressway for the 25 miles to Jerusalem.

As in past years, we made our residence with the Sisters of Zion at the Center for Biblical Study, located at the First Station of the Cross on the Via Dolorosa (the Sorrowful Way). Through our ten-day stay, the temperatures hovered in the middle 60°F, an unbelievable happening in the usually cold winter climate of mountainous Jerusalem. Each morning, on coming out of my warm, comfortable room (night temperatures in 40°F) to the 3rd floor balcony, I saw the sun coming up over the Mount of Olives.

As I looked out over the Old City, built on the side of a mountain and only six blocks square, a blessed quietness and peace filled the sweet air. Just a hundred yards away stands the famous Wailing Wall (the original West Wall of the Temple in the time of Christ), the center of prayer for the Jewish people. Next to it, overlooking the Wall and its huge, open plaza, is the Mosque Al-Asque with its bright golden dome, the place of worship for the Muslim community. Farther up the mountainside, about three blocks away to the west, I noticed the Church of the Holy Sepulcher, the holiest shrine in Christendom, built around AD 300. Mount Calvary and the Tomb of Christ lie under its roof. A pilgrim in Jerusalem immediately sees the importance of God and prayer.

Friday, January 3, 1997. On this morning, I am offering 7:00 am Mass in our residence, in its lower level, a place acclaimed by all scholars as the actual courtyard of Pilate. My two lay friends, Captain Jack, a Southwest Airlines pilot, and Tom, a lawyer from Albuquerque, New Mexico, stand at the altar with me in the perfect silence of this holy place. We are conscious of the many humiliations Jesus received on this very ground many years ago. At Communion time, I tell the Lord I am determined not to sadden Him further by any sins in my life, even the slightest kind. As St. Paul wrote, "Keep yourself pure, holy and

*A pilgrim in Jerusalem immediately sees the importance of God and prayer.*

unspotted from this world."

Years ago, Bishop James Pike, an Episcopalian prelate, died from dehydration in the nearby desert. An author of many inspiring books on the person of Jesus, this hero of mine always came to Jerusalem before he wrote one of these books to "drink in the spirit of Jesus." Next to his body, in the desert, rescuers found knee prints in the sand. In his last moments, the Bishop was reaching out to the Lord. I would like to die that way with my knee prints next to my body, in the sands or the dirt, searching for Christ. Is not this the purpose of Lent, to seek the close friendship of the Nazarean?

*Father McKenna offers Mass in the Chapel of the Sisters of Zion at the First Station of the Cross.*

# In The Holy Land 1994

Wednesday, February 9, 1994. A sunny, mild day. The Garden of Gethsemane lies just outside the walls of the Old City. I go to Mary's Grotto in the Garden to offer the Mass of the Betrayal of Jesus. This Grotto has a special attraction for me, a cave with a seven-foot ceiling and room for about thirty people. In the dark atmosphere, with the bare rock on all sides, I find this an ideal place to pray.

Behind the altar, a painting depicts Judas placing a kiss on the Master's cheek. The readings of this Mass bring home to me the evil of sin, its destructive qualities. After Mass, with no one present except the Franciscan Brother in charge, I sit down and make an hour of prayer. Here in this place, heartbreak came to the Lord as His follower, Judas, gave Him into the hands of His enemies. I beg the Lord not to let sin enter my life. "Death rather than sin"—the motto of my hero saint, John Bosco.

In another part of the Garden of Gethsemane, I come upon an outdoor Mass about to begin. Some 40 American priests on pilgrimage stand on the hillside around the altar. Alleluia! Another chance to join with fellow priests in celebrating Mass has come to me. To receive under Both Species. The priests with whom I feel an immediate closeness come in all sizes and ages. We pray the Holy Mysteries together, my prayer being for them, for their good health and spiritual wholeness. The thought comes, "I'm glad I am a priest."

Thursday, February 10, 1994. Off to Bethlehem this morning. A five-mile ride on a noisy Arab bus. One Israeli shekel (33 cents USA). On arrival at 9:00 am, I have a chance to make an hour of prayer in the Church of St. Catherine of Alexandria, immediately adjoining the Basilica of the Nativity. Some years ago, I was pastor of a church in Oak Lawn, Illinois, by this same name, St. Catherine of Alexandria. My prayers in the cold, damp church ask God to bless all the people of that parish. I am the Pastor Emeritus there.

*All their joy flows into my heart, too. An unexpected bonus for me*

At 10:30 am, I stand at the altar in the Grotto of the Nativity, with room there for about twenty people. This morning I am alone as I joyfully offer the Mass of Christmas. The Lord comes down on the altar as He did in this very neighborhood 2000 years ago. How peaceful and still are the surroundings in the Grotto Chapel!

Afterwards, an American group enters the cell of

St. Jerome, next to the Grotto. Only forty-two people can fit into this chapel for Mass. I am the 42nd. A charismatic group, with three priests, celebrates the Mass. The Spirit-filled assembly proclaim the Goodness of the Lord. All their joy flows into my heart, too—an unexpected bonus for me. "O little town of Bethlehem!" Why did the Savior choose you for His birthplace? The Lord always blesses the lowly.

*A view from the top of the Mount of Olives,
looking toward the Old City.*

# Mary Meant Much
# To The People Of The Middle Ages

While visiting five magnificent cathedrals in France this past September 1997, I made an amazing discovery! Through love of Mary, the builders and townsfolk dedicated these mighty Houses of Worship to Our Lady, the Mother of God. Notre Dame de Rouen (Our Lady of Rouen), Notre Dame de Rheims, Notre Dame de Evreux, Notre Dame de Chartres and Notre Dame de Paris. This last Cathedral (my favorite) took 100 years to build.

Back in the Middle Ages, the 12th, 13th and 14th centuries, the pennies of the peasants went to putting up these colossal structures in their towns. Even today, these churches stand out above all other buildings in their respective cities, so high and elegant are they. In those times of the Middle Ages, the people of France saw Mary as the channel through which all graces come to Earth. All the cathedrals are still in excellent condition!

On a Thursday afternoon, September 25, 1997, I was praying in the mighty Cathedral of Chartres, built in AD 1120 over 100 years, the largest in France and

75 miles south of Paris. I found much inspiration in picturing the crowds of young people there on pilgrimage in the 12th, 13th and 14th centuries. Historians call the 13th century the greatest of all centuries. Stories from that time (Chaucer's *Canterbury Tales*) tell of the faith-filled young men and women tramping 75 miles from Paris to pray and leave their requests in Mary's hands!

I closed my eyes and saw them marching along the roads, a five-day journey, with their banners flying aloft, singing Marian hymns, attending Mass in wayside chapels, accepting bread from farmers. Truly, that was an age of faith! These followers of Our Lady showed a wholesome excitement and remarkable faith in Mary's place in their spiritual life. She had a place in their families, a chair at their tables, a person of powerful love for each one of them!

*These followers of Our Lady showed a wholesome excitement and remarkable faith in Mary's place in their spiritual life.*

A year ago, my brother gave me a statue of Our Lady about 18 inches high, Our Lady of the Miraculous Medal. Since my experience at Chartres, some months ago, I have tried to inject more enthusiasm and faith into my devotion to Mary. I placed the appealing statue of Our Lady on my bedroom dresser. I can look into her face and lay before her with total confidence all my hopes and plans for life.

This attitude of sharing my daily life adds excitement to my devotion to Mary. All of us can make our love for Mary so much more adventure-filled and thrilling, if we added a good dose of enthusiasm! Remember the youth of the 13th century!

*Front entrance of the Notre Dame de Rheims Cathedral in France.*

# I Offer Mass At The Sixth Station Of The Cross For The First Time

Jerusalem, January 5, 1996, Saturday. Not a warm day but rather brisk with temperatures in the lower 50°F. I walk alone to the Sixth Station of the Cross, where Veronica wiped the Face of Jesus. In thanks, the suffering Christ left His Image on her towel. The other five pilgrims in our group have left early for a ride to the North, to Nazareth and the Sea of Galilee.

At the Sixth Station, the Little Sisters of Jesus, a group founded by Charles Faucould, a Frenchman, have a small shop with religious articles for sale, a means of supporting their community. In years past, I always went there to give them an offering of money with a request for prayers for a safe pilgrimage. Until a few days ago, I never knew they had a chapel next to their store.

While in the shop at that time, I heard a door open, and there before me I saw a cave-like chapel, some six feet below the pathway outside! At that level, I was looking at the Jerusalem of the time of Jesus. In this place, the Lord met Veronica and accepted her loving action!

On this Saturday morning, the Sisters are expecting me, since I had reserved a time to celebrate Mass.

When the three German priests had finished celebrating Mass and come into the sacristy, they offered me warm salutations, *"Guden Tag."* The world fraternity of priests creates a wonderful bond between all priests wherever they meet. I responded in my best German. A smile is understood in all languages. With my heart beating rapidly, with no one present in the chapel with its capacity of 40 worshippers, I vested and approached the altar to offer Mass. If only young men knew the joys of being a priest.

After Mass, in my thanksgiving, I thought of the consolation Veronica gave to the bruised and bloody Face of Christ as He struggled up the steep roadway to Calvary. Before this, I had never prayed to Veronica, although her name came up frequently during the Lenten Season each year. In the days since my Mass at the Sixth Station, she has become a dear friend to me. I beg her often in prayer to help me offer consolation to our Christ of the 20th century. She has made me conscious of many different ways.

> *After Mass, in my thanksgiving, I thought of the consolation Veronica gave to the bruised and bloody Face of Christ as He struggled up the steep roadway to Calvary.*

In our striving for holiness, our lives can give much praise and love to Christ, offended by so much indifference and rejection at the present stage of world history. Why aren't our churches filled to overflowing on weekends? Perhaps Veronica will mean more to us, when we appreciate her courage and love in showing public devotion to a condemned Man.

Stand up for Christ in the marketplace, at home, in our local church! Ask Veronica to inspire us with her zeal and love for the Forgotten Lord!

*One of the many quaint and picturesque streets in Jerusalem.*

# Pilgrimage To The
# Monastery Of Padre Pio

April 18, 1997, Friday, Rome, Italy. After finishing the four-day Catholic Airport Chaplains Seminar in the countryside, I come back to Rome and its chaotic traffic. With three friends, I plan to drive south for some six hours to visit Giovanni Rotondo, the monastery town of Padre Pio (1885-1968). Before we opened the chapel in Midway Airport, I prayed for 18 months to this holy Capuchin priest to help us accomplish this "dream."

Born Joseph Forgione in Pietrelcina, a small town south of Rome, he entered the Capuchin (Franciscan) Order as an unlikely candidate, because of his poor health. However, he showed himself a giant in his faith in prayer. One day while praying before a crucifix in 1919, he received the stigmata, the five wounds of Christ, in his hands, side and feet. For the next many years, until his death, Padre Pio (his name in religion) bore the pain of these open sores patiently. For ten years he was forbidden by Rome from preaching or celebrating Mass publicly. More suffering for him.

Even while Padre Pio was alive, crowds of pilgrims started coming to his small, isolated monastery town of Giovanni Rotondo to attend his Masses and confess their sins. In a spirit of thanksgiving for his help to us at Midway Airport, we four drive to the south this Friday afternoon. Late at night, we stop in City of Foggia at a small hotel for a spaghetti and steak supper—also to sleep.

April 19, 1997, Saturday. Huge numbers of pilgrims fill the streets in Giovanni Rotondo. Fortunately, I am able to celebrate Mass at the Tomb of the holy priest at 7:00 in the evening, a wondrous and cherished experience! One of our four speaks fluent Italian, a gift that makes our travels a joy. With his help, we arrange for a Mass on the next day at 6:00 am on Padre Pio's daily Mass altar in the old church (Antica Chiesa), seating capacity about a hundred.

*For ten years he was forbidden by Rome from preaching or celebrating Mass publicly.*

April 20, 1997, Sunday, 5:30 am. All four of our group admit our hearts are beating out a new song of happiness at this pilgrimage in honor of Padre Pio, whose photo hangs in our Midway Airport Chapel. To our surprise, pilgrims fill the streets at this early hour on their way to the great Basilica to attend Mass. I feel humble and dismayed as I begin Mass on this altar where usually Padre Pio took two and three hours to celebrate the Divine Mysteries. How much more deeply he treasured the Mass! Yesterday, I spent some hours in this old church, asking my patron, Padre Pio, to help me love the Mass more.

April 21, 1997, Monday, 7:00 am, Rome. We stay in a *pension* (small hotel) within the shadow of St. Peter's Basilica last night. In five minutes we walk through the rain to offer Mass in St. Peter's. To enter this great Church of Christendom is truly awesome. I celebrate Mass at the tomb of St. Leo the Great (died AD 461), a fitting end to eight shining days in Italy. Alitalia Flight #684 brings us home to Chicago on this Monday afternoon.

*Padre Pio offering Mass.*

# The Need For Mothers

T he Louvre in Paris, France, ranks among the top three outstanding art museums in the world. Its sprawling four-story buildings cover many acres on the Left Bank of the Seine River, almost in sight of the Notre Dame (Our Lady) Cathedral. Years ago, on my first visits to this treasure house of art, I discovered a number of galleries devoted entirely to paintings and sculpture works of Mary, the Mother of Christ. In these large galleries or halls, reaching up to a height of forty feet, hang the works of artists of the last 1000 years who had tried to portray the beauty and holiness of Our Lady.

Among these, I saw one creative piece of art that gripped my heart. In a traditional setting, Mary sat on a chair with her left arm wrapped around the Holy Child as He sat on her knee. Then came the unusual twist to this work of art. A dirty, ragged street child, a boy or girl, knelt before her. Our Lady, with a loving glance, had extended her right hand to touch the head of this youngster.

Mary was saying, "Yes, I love my Child, Jesus, but I care as much for this child not loved by anyone. They are both precious to me." We, children of Mary, see ourselves in that dirty-faced youngster. As we kneel before our mother, Mary, with all our weaknesses, her love warms our hearts.

One day, I saw a repeat of this painting in the loving actions of a young mother on the Metro, the Paris subway. Across the aisle from me sat a mother with her little son and daughter, about four and five. Suddenly, the little boy began striking his sister, then flung his well-taped wire rim glasses on the seat and fell to the floor, screaming loudly. Rush-hour commuters jammed the aisles.

I will never forget the performance of the mother, no violent threats or actions on her part. She silently reached out her long, slender hand to her troubled son with a look of gentle love. Nothing more than that! Shortly, the boy came to his mother for her embrace, an unforgettable experience of a mother's love.

Even though we age with years, we remain children at heart. As children, we could scream out our frustrations and fears of the unknown. As adults, we must conform to society's standards and keep these hurts and fears

*As we kneel before our mother, Mary, … her love warms our hearts.*

bottled up within ourselves with much harm to our emotional life! We need a mother of love to approach and confide in! Our Lady will reach out her open arms to us where we can find peace.

# Our Two Mothers

In His Love for us, God has given us two mothers, one earthly and the other heavenly. My earthly mother's name was Mary, so I have two mothers named Mary. Both have loved me beyond all that words can describe. In all languages, the word *Mother* comes across as the sweetest of all. What endearing thoughts fill our minds when we hear it spoken—love without limits, unselfishness, devotion, gentleness, a willingness to die so that new life could see the light of day.

We could have come into the world like apples or watermelons, a cold entrance into a cold world. In His Wisdom, God devised a marvelous way for human life to be born. Before birth, we were to spend nine months in our mother's womb—a warm, peaceful place, taking nourishment from her, listening to the reassuring thump-thump of her heart. In these months, our mothers fell in love with us, even before seeing us. On giving birth—with its pains—their hearts rejoiced with a joy beyond all telling.

Think of all the love we have received from our two mothers. When as infants we were totally dependent on them, they watched over us with care beyond measure, 24 hours a day! We learned the first lessons of life from them—how to love others, to pray, to practice good manners. As a boy, my mother would tell me to make the sign of the cross before going out the door to school, or to play. Through the years, I still make the sign of the cross as I leave my home.

In our days as children, when tears were always close to our eyes from life's painful happenings, we ran to our mother's arms for comfort and solace. Never did we hear, "Come back tomorrow." Rather, her arms were always open for loving hugs. God made mothers' hearts in a special way to love without limit. It was apparent to me that my mother, an immigrant from County Mayo, Ireland, at age of 17, loved Mary, the Mother of Christ. Through the day her rosary was always close to her fingers. Is that why, today, I love Mary, too?

*What would our mothers wish for us today: riches, a place of power in the world, many possessions?*

What would our mothers wish for us today: riches, a place of power in the world, many possessions? No! If they, living or dead, stood before us, they would cry out, "Be honest, pure and loving people, respectful of others, prayerful, honoring God with weekend worship!" With this lifestyle, we can show both our mothers our love, respect and gratitude for all their care for us! It's not too late for any of us to make this our way of life!

For the first twenty-one years of my priesthood, I phoned my mother every night. As time went on, I said to myself, "Some night, I will not hear that sweet voice answering my call." My father had died many years before. At my mother's passing, I was devastated. In a short time, I will lie next to her in Holy Sepulcher Cemetery. At the present time, I still think of my earthly mother Mary every day and ask my Heavenly Mother Mary to take care of her.

# The Man Who Defied Death

In his wonderful book, *The Anatomy Of An Illness,* Norman Cousins told how laughter and cheerfulness brought him back from the brink of death. As Editor of the *Saturday Review,* a high quality literary magazine, Cousins enjoyed much prestige. One day, the doctors told him he had 1 in 500 chances to survive a sudden cancer that attacked his body.

With the help of his faithful doctor, Norman left the hospital and set up his own regimen of treatment. With the Marx Brothers' movies, joke books, humor magazines, old time comedies, he concentrated on a diet of laughter, cheerfulness and a spirit of lightheartedness. After many laughs, he found that he could sleep soundly for several hours, something he found impossible to do in the months before. This good sleep helped his weakened body.

Contrary to all expectations, excellent health came back to Cousins. The world of medicine sat up and began to investigate the place of good humor and cheerfulness in the treatment of sick people.

A girl phoned Norman Cousins. "What can I do to help myself?" The increasing paralysis in her legs had brought the whole family to a state of desolation. Sadness, anxiety and silent wailing filled the house with a devastating gloom which only increased the dark spirits of the girl. Cousins told the family to go to the library and find old comedies and books on humor. "Of course, continue your medical treatments!"

Immediately, the spirit of the house changed for the better. A lightheartedness crept in the back door, with laughter frequently heard, and even singing. All this had a definite effect on the ailing girl, who took time each day to phone Cousins with her favorite joke of the day.

> *A lightheartedness crept in the back door, with laughter frequently heard, and even singing.*

What has the above to do with the reader's place in life? Perhaps we live in a house of tension. This can be even if we live alone. Angry voices, long faces, little merriment and rare laughter make up the daily menu of our home. With such an atmosphere, we not only miss out on the healing powers of cheerfulness, but we can bring real physical harm to the physical structure of the body. I smile often to myself, even in times of darkness. Something good happens!

In my last visit to Jerusalem, in January 1995, I enjoyed my best pilgrimage by far. On looking back to find out the reason, I realized the companionship of my four lay friends made the big difference. We laughed much at all our meals, made light of our difficulties and treated each other with love and respect. We weren't afraid to share our life stories with each other in order to give each other hope for the days ahead.

# Happiness Only Comes From Within

For the first 25 years of my priesthood (1944–69), I served the Chicago Archdiocese as a full-time teacher of youth. It all began at Maryville Academy in Des Plaines, at that time a year-round home for 850 children, nursery age to high school seniors, aptly named "The City Of Youth." After a five-year assignment there, I went on to 20 years as a teacher at Quigley Seminary, a training ground for future priests, all youngsters of high school age. I never foresaw all this!

Right away, I chose St. John Bosco (1815–1888), the Apostle of Youth, as my favorite Saint. I read and re-read every biography of his printed to help me in the difficult work of helping young people grow into living images of the Lord. In his time, in Turin, Italy, a northern industrial city, Don (Father) Bosco took boys off the streets and prepared them for life. In his daily talks to his children, Don Bosco often repeated his favorite maxim. "There is no happiness in sin." I traveled to Turin a number of times!

I found myself repeating his words to the youngsters I taught! We are always seeking happiness. Every choice we make, whether we realize it or not, is based on our pursuit of happiness, fulfillment and contentment. Some examples of these choices would be the food we buy, the work we choose to do, the man or woman we take as our husband or wife, and the school we attend.

In life, the World, the Flesh, and the Devil offer us many choices, most of them against God's Will for us: pleasure, dishonest money, broken vows, addictive drugs. If we accept these forbidden things, we bring much unhappiness into our hearts. Cry out, "There is no happiness in sin!" I personally found this saying a powerful means

*Happiness isn't found in our big house, the cars in the driveway, the generous bank account, the companionship of other men and woman.*

of turning from these attractive and alluring choices. The true picture of my search for happiness becomes evident.

Happiness comes from within! It's an inside job! Happiness isn't found in our big house, the cars in the driveway, the generous bank account, the companionship of other men and women. Happiness springs from our heart! My favorite Beatitude is: "Happy are they who hunger and thirst for holiness. They shall have their fill." What a helpful custom to say this often to ourselves!

If we are unhappy, discontented with life, despairing—refuse to blame this on "someone or something out there!" Happiness comes from within! Perhaps, we are making the wrong choices. "There is no happiness in sin." I pray that my former students are using this in their search for peace.

*Erin O'Donnell, Deputy Commissioner of Aviation,*
*giving Father McKenna a plaque from Mayor Richard M. Daley,*
*congratulating him on his eightieth birthday.*

# My Amsterdam Experience

One morning, some years ago in Amsterdam, Holland, I disembarked in the Central Railroad Station and walked out through its doors into the busy square. Electric trolley cars moved up and down the many avenues leading to the station. Later in the day, I would board one of these narrow cars for a quick trip around this famous city where Anne Frank lived during World War II.

In the distance, several blocks away, a tall church spire lifted itself to the gray, dark sky. In my mind, this would be the first goal I would seek out. Dodging the trolley cars and the fast moving traffic, I set out across the many thoroughfares to visit this church, so close to the center of the city's activities.

This could be an especially exquisite place of worship, an enduring memory to carry away with me from this old Dutch City of Amsterdam. I had set my expectations high! Finally, I arrived at the front of the church. Only four steps led from the sidewalk to its front doors.

Across the entrance way ran a badly scarred, metal picket fence. Loose papers, broken bottles and other kinds of rubbish littered the steps of this once elegant entrance. No one had used the church for years. I have never seen a more tragic sight!

With a sigh of disappointment, I took the long walk back to the City Square. Many thoughts came to me. A person's soul resembles a church, where God receives praise and honor. If one could look into one's inner spirit, would one see a breathtaking spectacle, a holy place brightly lit with prayer and holiness of life? Would the steps be clean and freshly scrubbed from the frequent visits of this person into the inner spirit in prayer?

What picture does one's soul present to God? Does the Lord come upon this place of worship and, to His disappointment, see the dust and decay of neglect, the litter of bad habits cluttering the entrance way, the iron gates of a hardened heart, no longer opening to God's visits?

*A person's soul resembles a church, where God receives praise and honor.*

My experience in Amsterdam has encouraged me to keep an eye on my soul, where lives the Holy Spirit of God. When tempted to compromise my ideals and commitment to God, I have remembered the front doors of the abandoned Church. Suddenly, I take new courage to keep beautiful my inner House of Worship out of respect for the All-Holy God.

# A Guide Beyond All Compare

As often as possible, I make solo trips through the Art Museum on Michigan Avenue in downtown Chicago, always with the hope that some of the culture in this House of Treasures will rub off on me. At times, I come across groups of young children, sitting on low stools before a painting and listening to a trained museum guide.

Usually a woman, the guide, with a pleasing, cultured voice, explains many features of the work of art to the youngsters. A sadness comes over me as I realize how much I am missing by making this museum visit alone, with my meager knowledge of art.

My thoughts move on to life itself. My walks through the galleries of the museum compare with my travels through my daily living. I rush along alone with little knowledge of life. The events of each day are similar to the works of art hanging in the galleries. Oftentimes, these happenings in daily life cause me much heartache and pain because I don't understand them.

If only I had an expert person like the museum guide to draw more riches from these "masterpieces" in life! I do have such a person in the Holy Spirit. Jesus says, "I will give you the Holy Spirit Who will explain all things to you." I picture the Spirit as a young Person, full of love for me, terribly interested in bringing joy and peace to my life.

Consider some of the many "masterpieces" filling the walls in the galleries which I call my daily life. I look on many of these as painful unemployment, a dark depression of the mind, a disgust with life, a strong desire to give up on God, the breaking of a relationship, a long sickness in the family, a personal illness, moral faults.

At my faith-filled request, my Loving Friend, the Spirit of God, will approach the "masterpiece" and in clear, simple language explain this happening in my life, how I can enrich myself from this distressing experience. No more solo flights through life for me, not when I can have this Super-Intelligent Guide, the Holy Spirit, as my Companion.

*Oftentimes, these happenings in daily life cause me much heartache and pain.*

A few nights ago, a woman with a distressful tone in her voice phoned me, asking for prayers. Evidently, some tragic things had come into her life, and she was trying to make a new start. She mentioned the Holy Spirit. I was delighted to hear that! With the Spirit, success was certain to come!

# John The Baptist
# Led People To Christ

One modern John the Baptist stands out in my life. His name, coincidentally, was John, too—Father John Hinsvark. Back in 1976, I lived with this priest in Bethel, Alaska, a community of 3,500 people, of whom 70% were Eskimos. About 500 miles west of Anchorage, with no roads in between, Bethel and its jet airport stood as the largest community in the far west of Alaska. Among the 38 priests in the Fairbanks Diocese, John and I were the only two diocesan priests, the others being Jesuits, including the Bishop.

Pleasant, lighthearted, generous in his words of encouragement, Father John overlooked my weaknesses and shared his wide knowledge of Eskimo life and culture with me. Ten years my junior, already 20 years in Alaska when I arrived on the scene, this physically strong man accepted me warmly and made me feel wanted and important.

What I found most appealing in my days with him was the predictability of his behavior. Day in and day out, my new found friend had few highs and lows, no swings of moods. No matter what happened, he remained kind, considerate, even-tempered, patient. His closeness to Christ, his belief in prayer, helped him to live this way. After a time, I began saying to myself, if Christ is helping him to be this kind of person, I want to know this Christ better, more intimately.

Even now, 22 years later, Father John's way of life still influences my actions. In Bethel, the Eskimos cherished his presence. At this time, in 1998, he is working in a remote Eskimo village on the Bering Sea. I assure myself, if I stay in close union with Christ each day, I, too, can be cheerful, in good spirits, supportive of others with me on the Glory Road. Thank You, Lord, for bringing this great-hearted person into my life, a John the Baptist for me!

*I assure myself, if I stay in close union with Christ each day, I, too, can be cheerful, in good spirits, supportive of others with me on the Glory Road.*

In God's Providence, all of us have the calling to be modern-day John the Baptists. What can prevent us from being loving people in our homes, our places of work and in our Community? Be nice people with those about us! Without our knowing it, we can have people saying: "Why is this person so kind, pleasant, helpful? Is it Christ Who helps him/her to act in this way? If that's the case, I want to bring Christ into my life through prayer.

Start out in the morning with a plan of action in our minds. When unexpected things happen, we will be ready to respond in a patient, even-tempered way as Christ would do. Lead others to the Lord!

# Jesus Asks, How Is Life Treating You?

The Risen Lord at the seashore, helping the sad Apostles bring in a great catch of fish, reminds me of an adventure in my life. About thirteen years ago, I found myself in Paris, France, much in the same spirit of the Apostles, bewildered, despondent and not in the best of health. My assignment to a parish had ended on a sour note, because of many unpleasant circumstances.

Every night, in the Chapel of the Foyer Sacerdotal in Paris, a residence for priests passing through the city, I sat in the semi-darkness, bitterly disappointed with life and downhearted. My health had turned shaky from all the tension of confrontations with people and the Bishop. There in the evenings, I saw the Lord standing, as He did on the seashore after the Resurrection. "It is the Lord," I said to myself. The Gentle Christ broke the ice with His question of concern, "How is it going, George?"

I told the Risen Lord about the three "H's" I needed badly: Home, Hope and Health. The darkness in my mind slowly went away. Back in Chicago, I came to a little parish down the street from Midway Airport,

Our Lady of the Snows. The rectory consisted of two bungalows, one for me and one for the pastor. I was to live in a real Home, not an institutional building. In this neighborhood of peace, the kindness of my fellow priests and the love of the people brought into my life a fresh surge of Hope for the future and a new delight to be alive. Soon, my frequent walks around the airport and the neighborhood were taking me six and seven miles, and with this exercise came good physical Health.

At the seashore, the once gloomy Apostles hauled in 157 large fish at the direction of the Risen Christ. What a display of generosity the Lord showed to raise up the spirits of His followers! In the same way, He picked me up far beyond my dreams!

*"How is it going?" Jesus says to each one of us as we try to cope with the trials of living.*

"How is it going?" Jesus says to each one of us as we try to cope with the trials of living. In faith we cry out, "It is the Lord." "Are you succeeding in life?" He calls out to us. Perhaps many readers have labored long and hard, but peace of heart, happiness and success in living eludes them! As He did to the Apostles on the seashore, the Lord will give directions for making dreams come true. Spell out exactly what you desire, as I did!

At that visit to the Lake of Galilee, the Master changed Peter's life by making him the First Pope! He can change our lives, too, by giving us a brighter outlook on life, a more cheerful acceptance of crosses, a new delight in prayer. We need to recognize Him as the Risen Lord and listen for His words.

# In The Land Of Christ 1994

February 5, 1994, Saturday Mass at Bethany. The Arab bus drops me off at this 2000-year-old community, just three miles from Jerusalem. The most recent church, built in 1935, seats seventy worshippers. As I vest for Mass in this sacred place, my heart beats faster with the realization of how often Jesus visited here with the family of Martha, Mary and Lazarus.

In the Mass, the Gospel tells of Jesus calling back Lazarus to life, "Come forth, Lazarus." On the side walls, paintings portray this miracle of resurrection, an event which sealed the fate of the Lord. Always, at Bethany, my prayer begs the Lord to raise me from the death of the spirit, to give me a resurrection unto a full life of peace and joy.

I picture the Lord saying to me, "Unwrap the burial cloths from this priest. Come forth, George, and enjoy fullness of new life." Large crowds of pilgrims come and, reluctantly, I leave Bethany to avoid the noise. My parting prayer is "Lord, please accept my presence as my heartfelt offering to You." Jesus wishes to free His friends from the darkness and desolation of their self-made tombs.

Outside the church, I copy in my notebook the words from a plaque on the wall. "One thing is needful and Mary has chosen the better part. Today, as in the past, the Love of Jesus seeks a refuge where He is lovingly expected and where He can rest. He finds our hearts filled with distractions—people, work, our own interests. He longs for us to empty our hearts and lovingly receive Him."

Wednesday, February 2, 1994. Mass at the Cenacle Chapel on Mt. Zion, just fifty yards away from the Last Supper Room. I feel many deep emotions as I say the words, "This is My Body. This is My Blood," at the Consecration time of the Mass. Christ first said those words a short way from this chapel, 2000 years ago. I am carrying out His wish, "Do this in memory of Me." A few days later, I come back to this little church, to its

*How powerful a force for good the Mass can be, I think to myself.*

semi-darkness, to pray for a greater appreciation of the Mass and the Eucharist. As Cardinal Newman said, "It is the Mass that matters." Twelve German priests stand around the altar celebrating Mass, so like the Last Supper. How powerful a force for good the Mass can be, I think to myself.

Thursday, February 3, 1994. Mass at the Flagellation Chapel at the beginning of the Via Dolorosa, The Sorrowful Way. It's another small chapel with places for about thirty people, with stained glass windows and exquisite marble altar. Above the altar an artist shows Christ tied to a pillar with soldiers whipping Him. He suffers for the sins of the flesh. My mind, here in Chicago, frequently goes back to this scene. Discipline the body!

*Tom Mescall visits the Wailing Wall in Old City, Jerusalem.*

# Give To God What Is God's

A while ago, in mid-October 1996, I received a letter from a priest friend, living in Connecticut on the East Coast. Ordained just five years ago at the age of 55, my friend of twenty years told me of his recent appointment as pastor to a parish in a small town with a population of 5000. In his letter, he enclosed the program booklet used at the Sunday Mass of his installation as pastor.

Before the Bishop of the Connecticut Diocese finally accepted him, my friend received many rejections from Bishops throughout the USA. I kept writing letters of recommendation. Because of the encouragement I had always given him to be a priest, I looked upon my friend as my spiritual son.

In part, the letter read: "I'm the only priest here, so I am kept busy. I have difficulty in saying my Breviary. No time." The Divine Office (Duty), called the Breviary, takes about 40 minutes to say, with prayers for morning, afternoon, evening and nighttime. The four books of the Office, in keeping with the four Liturgical Seasons of the Church Year, are mostly composed of Psalms of praise, thanks, petition and sorrow for sin. Priests, throughout the world, say these inspiring prayers every day for their people, for their welfare.

I wrote back to my friend. "Your words, 'no time for the Breviary,' set off alarm bells in my mind. The chief work of the priest has always been to pray for his people through the Mass and the Breviary. Get up before your people and tell them. I have been given too many things to do. My prayer life is disappearing. I will have to stop some of my activities so that I will be a worthwhile priest for you."

Then I said to him personally: "If you give your daily life to total activity without prayer, you will soon burn out, become a cranky old man, angry at your people for making so many demands on your time, and possibly lose interest in your priesthood. Be ruthless in crossing off activities that keep you from prayer! Every day, go over to church, say your Office reverently. Spend time there in the Presence of the Lord. Your words and messages to your 550 families will have a heavenly unction and divine inspiration."

*Be ruthless in crossing off activities that keep you from prayer.*

We must be convinced of the time we owe to God in prayers of thanks, praise, petition and sorrow for our sins. Days without a good measure of prayer can bring a despairing boredom to life. Things will upset us easily. We lose our "cool" as it were. Our personal weaknesses can easily overcome us. We owe God our expression of prayer, especially, the greatest of all prayers, Holy Mass, on the weekend Sabbath. We can talk to God in any position, walking, standing, sitting or kneeling.

I wasn't preaching to my priest friend. As my spiritual son, I wanted to spare him the mistakes I made as a new pastor.

# What Would Jesus Do
# If He Were In My Place?

E arlier in this month of November 1996, I bought
a paperback novel with an astounding history, at
our local book store for $2.49. First published around
1900, *In His Steps* now has sold 15 million copies, in
second place only to the Bible. Imagine a book still
on the shelves after 100 years! I have read and reread
this story many times over the years, always with a re-
freshing delight.

Charles Sheldon, the author, begins his novel with
the minister of a church offering a challenge to his
well-to-do congregation on a Sunday morning. Dr.
Maxwell, the clergyman, asks them to put this question before themselves as they make decisions each
day, "What would Jesus do if He were in my place?"

"Do this for a year," he urges them. *In His Steps* goes
on to tell of four people in the congregation and their
experiences in living out this question. Many others
took this challenge to heart, but the novel tells only
of the four mentioned: a newspaper man, a superin-
tendent in the railroad yards, a woman concert singer,
and a successful merchant. Although the background

of the story lies in the year around 1900 AD, I always found *In His Steps* an exciting and uplifting story, able to send my wishes "to walk in His footsteps" soaring.

How to explain the long-standing popularity of this book? The story grabs the imagination of the readers and offers them a door to a richer and more thrilling walk in life. Within our hearts, we have a thirst, a desperate hunger for the ideals of Christ, a yearning to be a person of peace and holiness like Him. The simple question, "What would Jesus do?" provides a clear way to walk in His steps.

From hearing the Gospel stories so often, we know how Jesus dealt with many difficult situations. In everyday living we meet these same experiences and can face them with the attitudes Christ had. In following this program, we need feel no tension, nervousness or make it a complicated process. We just say with a loving heart, "What would Jesus do if He were in my place?" and act accordingly.

> *The story grabs the imagination of the readers and offers them a door to a richer and more thrilling walk in life.*

How quickly we would cleanse our inner spirit of all kinds of weaknesses, our selfishness, unjust anger, short temper, our unwillingness to give time to prayer, unhealthy fears about the past or future, and all our unloving ways of treating others. From my own experience, I can tell the reader that I never saw such a quick change in my life for the better than when I carried out this practice, "What would Jesus do?" Put this challenge on the refrigerator!

*Father McKenna offers Mass at the Midway Airport Chapel.*

# A Fortunate Wake-Up Call

A year ago this time, in November 1996, two friends of mine had a close brush with death on a Florida expressway. Tom and Noel, both residents of Albuquerque, New Mexico, had flown to Miami, Florida, to visit with Tom's daughter, a student at the University of Miami. Plane connections between these two cities call for much patience and time-consuming waits in airports. After dinner with his daughter, Tom, now without sleep for 24 hours, set out with Noel to drive to Cape Canaveral to witness the launch of a space shuttle at the Kennedy Center.

As they sped along the expressway at 65 mph, Tom began to fall asleep. The car drifted into the grassy mid-strip with the oncoming traffic only some feet away. Suddenly, Noel cried out, "Tom, wake up!" With that, Tom woke up and, superb driver that he is, he gradually eased the racing car back into the expressway. A few seconds more and both my friends would have perished in a head-on collision with autos in the on-coming lanes.

For the next few days, my two friends felt the shock

of the near tragedy. Understandably so! The ghost of Specter Death was putting his icy fingers on their shoulders. Noel and Tom accompanied me in my travels in France this past September 1997, with Tom acting as our driver in the chaotic traffic of Paris and its environs. Be assured, we three passengers kept talking to Tom to help him stay alert in our long auto rides. We stopped frequently for coffee!

In the Gospel for the First Sunday of Advent, we hear words of warning from Jesus. "Be on guard lest your spirits become bloated with indulgence. Be on the watch, pray constantly for the strength to escape whatever is in prospect." We are rushing along the Glory Road on our way to a launch site, our own personal one. At this spectacular happening, we will not be spectators but, rather, actually be part of the launch catching us up into outer space to our Judgment before God.

*"Be on guard lest your spirits become bloated with indulgence."*

On the Glory Road, we can find ourselves falling into a deadly sleepiness, a nirvana of ease and unconsciousness, drifting off the straight and narrow road to spiritual death and disaster. How easy for the fears, worries and distractions of life to weigh down our eyelids and make us indifferent to God's place in our lives. In Sweden, the law forbids billboards on highways because of their distracting influence on drivers. Unfortunately, the Glory Road we all travel has countless appeals to greed, selfishness, addictions.

At this Advent Time 1997, the Gentle, Loving Christ cries out to us, "Wake up. Reform your life." Enter into the spirit of this Season, sweep out of our spirits all forms of evil that can blind us to the Beauty and Wisdom of the Glory Road. Tom and Noel made it to the launch site.

# A Visit To Omaha Beach

This past September 30, 1997, our pilgrim group of three drove out of the City of Paris, France, into the Normandy country to the northwest to visit Omaha Beach, the D-Day invasion site of June 6, 1944, about a 175-mile ride. On coming into view of the American Cemetery, my friends stopped and could not speak for a long time.

Words cannot describe the row upon row of white stone crosses, stretching endlessly into the horizon, some 10,000 of them. On D-Day, these men faced withering fire from enemy machine guns placed on the bluff overlooking the shore. All young men in the prime of life, they were anxious to live, but the call to duty, with all its dangers, superceded all other matters. The crosses represent only a small number of the members of the Armed Forces killed in the opening days of the greatest military invasion of all time.

In this month of November, the time-honored month of the dead, we draw inspiration for life from our military dead. By their example, these fallen heroes remind us of the quality of courage and honor resting in the hearts of each one of us. The dead buried at Omaha Beach were the young people living down the block from us, just ordinary boys. I was ordained a priest on May 6, 1944, exactly a month before this carnage took place at Omaha Beach. If I had not been in the Seminary, I could well be lying beneath one of the white crosses.

Instead, God has given me a long life with the joys and sorrows found in every human existence. I give thanks for the opportunity to taste life from youth to old age, for the chance to know God better in all the happenings of life. For these men lying here in the silence and quiet at Omaha Beach, life was just opening up for them, like a fresh flower in the springtime. A cruel death cut short their dreams and hopes for the future.

*Instead, God has given me a long life with the joys and sorrows found in every human existence.*

What will I do with my life? In our mind's eye, as we contemplate the present Omaha Beach, the holy dwelling place of our fallen men, we would do well to ask ourselves that question. God has given us many days to live! We can pass these days in a selfish, complaining manner, preoccupied with the material things of life. On the other hand, we can seize each day as a precious gift and work for God's Honor and Glory!

Inspired by fallen heroes, we can purify our minds and hearts of selfish attitudes, knowing that the greatest victory is the victory over the evil within us. In our innermost hearts, we possess courage not only to rush enemy machine gun nests but, more importantly, to drive out addictions to evil in its many forms.

Seeing the American military cemeteries in France this past September 1997 has affected my life deeply. Call it a rich bonus I didn't foresee from my visit to France. As of now, I cannot tolerate a haphazard attitude towards life, allowing carelessness about God's Honor to take over my days.

*Father McKenna visits the American Military Cemetery in Belleau Woods, France.*

# O Death, Where Is Thy Victory, Where Is Thy Sting?

L ast month, in early October 1993, late on a Saturday evening, I went to the home of a good friend. Sick for the past year, Martin, my friend, had come to his last hours on Earth. Before the next dawn, his spirit would leave his mortal body and wing its way to the Heavenly Courts of God.

With his family gathered in the sick room, we began the lengthy prayers for a departing soul in an ideal setting. Fully alert to all that was taking place, Martin saw his five daughters and his son, all in their 30s, and his wife, ringing the bed on their knees. Their elbows rested on the bed spread. They had come to encourage their loved one in this last challenge of life.

At the end of the prayers, we recited the Litany of the Saints and asked these holy people to escort Martin on his way to the Throne of God. My friend, along with his family, received the Lord in the Holy Eucharist, the pledge of life everlasting. Afterwards, his wife, daughters and sons hugged him closely and spoke to him encouraging words of love and gratitude.

Through a lifetime of good example, my friend was leaving to his family the precious heritage of his Catholic Faith. May he rest in peace!

In many times past, I have mentioned my complete confidence in St. Joseph in my travels away from home. Over the years, in many places and ways, St. Joseph helped me find places to sleep out of the cold and darkness in strange cities, the right corners to turn. I know he will help me in my last journey, since he stands before me as the Patron of a Happy Death. Every day, my dear friend hears me say, "Dear St. Joseph, give me the grace of a peaceful death."

From all sides, we keep hearing the advice, "Prepare for life," especially directed to school children and students of all ages. Why don't we cry out a much better admonition, "Prepare for death," by building up a huge, heavenly bank account of good deeds and efforts to spread the Kingdom of Christ on Earth? Too gloomy and depressing a message, some would say. Those people, using this "war cry" every day, could tell of the joy and peace it brings. "Prepare for death."

*With his family gathered in the sick room, we began the lengthy prayers for a departing soul in an ideal setting.*

# The Beauty Of Graciousness

O n a past Saturday, September 6, 1997, the English people conducted funeral services for their Cinderella Princess Diana, affectionately called Princess Di. Never in present memory has England, as a nation, shown so much depth of emotion and sense of loss as it has for their young Princess. No one is trying to make her a saint, because, like us, she had her faults and weaknesses. However, all agree that the Princess possessed a rare, rich quality, the gift of graciousness.

This graciousness, radiant and vibrant, came from the respect and courtesy she showed to everyone she met, especially for suffering children. In the high level of English society and the Royal Family circle, Princess Di had a low rating because she mixed too much with the common people. According to their way of thinking, she didn't keep herself aloof enough from them. Of course, this trait of graciousness endeared her in a remarkable way with the English public. People began to think, maybe, that as a nation, we can be gracious to each other.

In His time, Jesus, the Prophet from Galilee, found

disfavor with the religious Institution, the Scribes and the Pharisees, since He associated with sinners and tax-collectors. In a recent Sunday Gospel, the Lord Jesus gave the gift of hearing to a non-Jew, a Gentile, something a good Jew would never dream of doing. The pages of the Gospels hold many such instances where Christ showed Himself as a gracious Human Being, kind and courteous.

At the end of her unhappy marriage, the young Diana refused to retreat into seclusion in bitterness, away from the public eye. Instead, she spear-headed causes for charity, among them: bringing attention to suffering AIDS victims and the elimination of land mines throughout the world. In her funeral procession, representatives from 110 charities, touched by her personal backing, marched in her honor.

*In His time, Jesus, the Prophet from Galilee, found disfavor with the religious Institution...*

In her tragic death, we can examine our own spirit of graciousness. How delightful to meet a person with this gift, one who puts us at ease and makes us feel important! I just finished speaking on the telephone with a hospital receptionist and an insurance interviewer, both women. Their voices, warm and unhurried, helped me solve my personal dilemma. Gracious people!

Each one of us can be a gracious person, treating all people we meet with love and respect, no matter what their station in life. On my recent travels to Sweden and France, I asked dozens of questions for information, always receiving courteous answers from the people of these countries. Make our homes and city, places where gracious living holds paramount importance. Who can stop us? "Here lies a gracious person." Will this be the epitaph on our gravestone? Eternal rest be given to Princess Diana!

# The Preciousness Of Our Catholic Faith

My father, Patrick, died in July 1936, and my mother, Mary, in October 1965. As young people, they came from Ireland on small, rickety ships, a terrifying experience, to seek their fortunes in the USA. With few worldly goods but rich in their beliefs of their Catholic Faith, they met here in Chicago and married. When we four children came along, three boys and a girl, we unconsciously absorbed their beliefs in our minds and hearts.

Seeing my father kneel at his bedside for his evening prayers made a lasting impression on me. He never told me to pray, but his actions spoke more loudly than words. Through the dark days of the 1920s and 1930s, my parents persevered in practicing their Faith, with worship on Sundays and with our education in Catholic schools. What a wonderful gift from God to me to grow up in a Catholic atmosphere! In difficult days, my mother spoke often of God's care for us and, also, the Blessed Mother's love for each one of us. Her rosary was never far from her fingers.

I knew many children on our block who had no

religious upbringing, no Church to attend on Sunday mornings. Through no fault of their own, they were missing out on precious gifts available to me on a daily basis. My First Communion told me that Jesus of Nazareth came to me in the White Host, to enrich my life with His Presence. If I broke the Commandments, the priest in Confession could forgive my sins. What a welcome relief to hear his forgiving words of absolution!

To be honest, at times I envied the other children on the block, whose families gave little attention to the practice of religion. While I had to stop and think of the Ten Commandments before I did things, they just went ahead and did whatever they wished. As time went on, I came to see the blessings of these guidelines to happiness. Keeping the Commandments was proof of my love for God. My Catholic Faith helped me through sicknesses, bewildering days of challenge, because I knew God was walking with me. Didn't my mother tell me this?

*Through no fault of their own, they were missing out on precious gifts available to me on a daily basis.*

Reading the Lives of the Saints meant much to me! As a caddy, carrying a golfer's bag, I often begged St. Anthony to help me find my player's golf ball in the high grass. He seldom failed me! I saw St. Joseph, often with a lily in his hand, a symbol of his purity of mind and heart. To be close to the Christ, I had to keep myself pure in thoughts and speech. St. Therese of Lisieux, Joan of Arc, John Vianney and John Bosco—all had messages of encouragement for me.

I will be eternally grateful to my mother and father for the Gift of my Catholic Faith.

# Time Marches On

January 1, 1996, New York City, John F. Kennedy Airport, New Year's Evening. About 400 people of all ages gather in a departure gate of the TWA terminal, waiting to board Flight 810, direct to Tel Aviv, slated to leave at 9:30 pm. One of our group of six, a young 35-year-old priest from Billings, Montana, decides to go down to the Japan Air terminal and view on TV the Notre Dame football game, taking place in Hawaii.

By 9:30 pm, all passengers had boarded the TWA 747 jet plane, except our young priest friend from Montana. Without Father Larry on board, the pilots would not leave the gate. The priest had checked luggage onto the flight back in O'Hare Airport that morning. Finally, at 10:30 pm, our missing man returned to the TWA terminal, bewildered at seeing the empty departure gate. Why was he so late? Unwittingly, he had left Montana time on his wristwatch, a two-hour difference from New York time (EST). We made Jerusalem safely the next day.

How necessary for us to keep track of time! Because of muddled thinking, we allow ourselves unlimited amounts of months and years ahead. For some people, that stretch of years suddenly ends—with unfulfilled dreams and future plans vanished. Even if life is not cut short, the days disappear like magic. Try to hold on to quicksilver or water flowing through the hands. An impossible mission! So, too, time can slip away from us.

"Some one of these days, I'm going to build a closer relationship with Jesus of Nazareth." "You and I will take that long desired trip soon." "A short time from now, I'll stop these 18-hour working days so that we can get on with our family life." "In the near future, I'll make up with my brother after these 20 years of silence." Perhaps the reader has heard these words coming from one's own mouth. Our watchword could be, "Just do it!"

*Because of muddled thinking, we allow ourselves unlimited amounts of months and years ahead.*

Several years ago, a popular movie, *Carpe Diem* (Seize The Day), caught the fancy of the public. In the film a young teacher, Robin Williams, urges his students to treasure the day at hand, to make use of the present moment. In writing this article, I personally benefited greatly. More than ever before, my putting off things as a way of life suddenly became clearer to me. Certainly, I was not seizing the day at hand but, rather, postponing actions until later dates.

Once upon a time, an elderly, overworked physician spoke to his best friend, "Let's take a slow freighter ship to South America." Hard-working and up in years, the friend, a lawyer, protested at first, "I'm too busy, too many things to do." In the end, he reluctantly agreed to the two-month trip on the water. Shortly after returning, the lawyer suffered a heart attack, making death only a few hours away. With almost his last words, he told his physician friend, "I'm glad we made that trip!"

# A World-Shaking Prayer

Someone may ask me, "What prayer has helped you the most in your fifty-three years as a priest, outside of the Mass and Holy Scripture?" The answer comes quickly to my mind. The Jesus Prayer stands out as the best and the most powerful. The prayer consists of a few words, spoken to God with the Holy Name of Jesus included.

What I like about this prayer, and many people have told me the same, is that it can be said quickly. "Jesus, help me." Quite impossible to be distracted while saying it. By using His Name, I draw closer to the Friendship of Christ. He doesn't live in the past but moves alongside of me as a Friend very much alive and present to me.

The Jesus Prayer brings the Power of the Lord into my being—His Strength, His Mercy, His Love and Forgiveness. He stands with me in my present, trying circumstances. No matter is too small to be considered for prayer. My prayer need not always be an asking prayer, sometimes I can just share my feelings about life with Jesus of Nazareth, my Brother. I can tell

Him of my hopes, visions and dreams for life. "Jesus, I wish to be a loving person like You."

By the end of the day, I have spoken many prayers with words I have never used before. This variety of words and ideas adds adventure to the whole process of prayer and my relationship with the Lord. The Jesus Prayer can take place anywhere, not just when I am in church or on my knees. When I am walking, working, washing dishes or driving my car, spontaneously, words can come to my lips with the Holy Name a part of them.

*The Jesus Prayer can take place anywhere, not just when I am in church or on my knees.*

Have we ever lived with someone who never used our first name? From week to week, I may hear my first name only a few times, if at all. This practice builds up a distance between me and the other person. I sense a coldness, and no lasting friendship takes place. After a while, we both move on to other places, soon to forget each other. With the Person of Jesus, if we frequently use His Name in a spirit of faith, a deep closeness grows up and our friendship flourishes.

The Name "Jesus" means "Savior." No other Name on earth can equal It in Power and Holiness. When the devils and evil spirits hear His Name, they shiver in fear and run fast from the one using It. All through my priesthood of fifty-three years, the Holy Name has never failed to bring me peace, consolation and inspiration. I hope my last words on Earth will be those from the Book of Revelation, written by the Apostle John, "Come, Lord Jesus."

*Father McKenna, giving one of his famous three minute homilies at the Midway Airport Chapel.*

# God Answers All Prayers

One day, back in 1933, Sister Angelista CSC, our 8th-Grade teacher at St. Theodore's School, brought five of us boys down six flights of stairs to the church. Sister, not a youngster, placed us in different parts of the church and told us to pray about our poor conduct in class. In the time given us, I mulled over my selfishness in bringing Sister Angelista up and down those long stairways. When Sister came back, I was still praying on my knees, asking God to give me some sense. I consider those minutes a watershed experience in my life, an occasion of a change of outlook on life. Prayer took on a preciousness. Sister Angelista came to my First Mass.

We need prayer as much as we need food, drink and air. I treasure prayer, conversation with God, the Father, the Son and the Holy Spirit, as the best of all gifts. In speaking to God, I enter into the Presence of These Three Holy Persons and share my thoughts and hopes with Them. Oftentimes, people lose interest in prayer because God has turned a deaf ear to them. So it seems.

Let the word go forth that God answers all prayers. This is not a matter, on God's part, of picking and choosing from all the prayers that rise to Heaven. Perhaps a few examples will make this good news clear. Suppose I have been praying for peace in the world. Nothing appears to happen! Unknown to me, in a home down the street from me, where every day loud and angry voices spilled out hateful words, a sudden stillness comes. The members of the family begin to respect each other. A lasting peace has come to a little piece of the world. God has answered my prayer!

Many of God's people suffer pain, exhausting sicknesses. Their plea to God begs the Almighty to take away all this discomfort, but often, the sick conditions stay as they are. Has God refused to hear their prayers? No! One morning, a new attitude of acceptance comes into the mind of the distraught patient. I will bear with this pain for the Love of God. Peace and courage fill the heart! These new insights come as an answer to prayer.

*We need prayer as much as we need food, drink and air.*

I, speaking for myself, personally, find this truth about God hearing and answering all prayers most consoling! When I am experiencing dark nights of the soul, I cry out, "Jesus, help me," again and again. How helpful to believe that those few words are flying into the Face of God! Gradually, peace and light fill my once disturbed spirit. In other words, no prayer is ever wasted. Thanks, praise, sorrow, petition.

Many times in 8th grade Sister Angelista encouraged me to think of the priesthood, but only in the final days of the school year did that way of life look inviting. Was Sister praying for me all through the year?

# Be An Encourager

What wonderful, encouraging letters St. Paul wrote to the churches from his prison in Rome! Death awaited him shortly, but he never fell into the trap of self-pity. "Live lives worthy of your calling. Be patient, humble." He passes over himself, his sad state, and exhorts his people to be mindful of their glorious destiny.

A child makes a crude gift. We respond, "O my, how wonderful!" Amazing what a word or action, done at the right time, can do to lift up the spirits of people about us. Their whole outlook on life can change because we spoke a word of brightness to them. From fifty years of experience in the priesthood, I conclude that people are more ready to concentrate on their weaknesses to the exclusion of their overwhelming successes.

Recently, at a celebration, I sat next to a friend whom I knew from a past parish I served in. She mentioned, "Years ago, when I went to confession to you and told you my weaknesses, you would always say, 'now, tell me about all your successes, all the good things you did.'" She went on to say, "This gave me much encouragement."

At an Airport Chapel Mass, I gave a test to the congregation by holding up a blank sheet of paper with a small dot in the center. I asked, "What do you see?" The vast majority responded, "I see a black dot." Only a few said, "A white piece of paper." In some way, this proves of how we emphasize our shortcomings and overlook the victories we have won. By our encouraging ways, we can help others see a full picture of their lives. They desperately need affirmations.

Overlook weaknesses! See all the good points of others. Bring these character pluses to the attention of the people we meet. Hug your children! Say often to those close to you, "Luv you!" About six years ago, in a homily at Our Lady of the Snows Church, I told the people of the sign that deaf persons use to say, "I love you." Three fingers are held up, the thumb, the forefinger and the small finger, while the two middle fingers are kept down. At my 50th Jubilee Mass, this past May 1st, 1994, at this same Church, I saw a friend holding up her hand, saying with sign language of the deaf, "I love you." She had remembered.

*Overlook weaknesses! See all the good points of others.*

# Use This Sign!

W hy be stingy with compliments? Give flowers to the living. "Encouragement" means "to put heart into someone." An aged man, dying alone in an open ward, liked a particular intern who worked on his floor. Why? Every time the young intern walked by his bed, he pinched the old man's big toe. Nothing was said, but recognition was given, "I know that you are there. Hang in there!" He died a peaceful death in Paris, 1997.

On a late Tuesday evening, September 23, 1997, a Scandinavian airliner (SAS) brought me to Paris, France, a 1000-mile journey from Stockholm, Sweden. I met my three lay friends in the Monastery of St. John Eudes in the heart of Paris. The next morning we drove through the bewildering traffic of the city towards Lisieux (pronounced LooSo), the home of St. Therese of the Child Jesus, about 100 miles away to the northwest.

On the way, we stopped at Evreux, an ancient cathedral town, to pray in its awesome church. One of my companions kept quoting a friend of his, "Who is This Person, Jesus Christ, that people built such great edifices in His Honor?" In the days ahead, we were to visit six of the greatest cathedrals in France. I heard that quotation often. At Lisieux, I offered Mass on the main floor of the huge Basilica at a side altar. We begged Therese to show us her "little way of holiness."

Thursday, September 25, found us in Chartres, 75 miles south of Paris, offering a pilgrimage of prayer to Mary in the largest cathedral in France, built around AD1000. In the Middle Ages, the young people of Paris walked these miles to Chartres in the springtime to leave their petitions with Mary. My good fortune helped me to offer Mass in the Crypt of this venerable edifice.

> *In the Middle Ages, the young people of Paris walked these miles to Chartres in the Springtime to leave their petitions with Mary.*

On Friday, September 26, we drove in our subcompact car to see the famous cathedral at Rouen (pronounced RuOn), about a three-hour ride straight north towards Belgium. One of our four weighs 250 pounds, lots of ballast. Words in print have no power to describe this splendid church. Again, a kind sacristan helped me to offer Mass at one of its great altars. In a side chapel, Our Lady of the Vow stands as a reminder of how Mary saved the people of Rouen from the plague in the 14th century.

On Saturday, September 27, our little band of pilgrims headed northeast to visit Rheims and its magnificent cathedral, built in the 12th century. What faith these people of the Middle Ages had to put up such a masterpiece of beauty! Just a mile away stands the place where Joan of Arc received the sentence to be burned at the stake. On our way home to Paris, we stopped off at Chateau-Thierry and Belleau Woods, two battlegrounds in World War I. How impressive the American Cemetery with its rows of white, stone crosses, the grass groomed immaculately! Eternal Rest grant unto them, O Lord! A name appears on each cross.

Sunday morning, September 28, we attended the Grand Mass in Notre Dame Cathedral, another structure of unbelievable Gothic beauty. In our rides, we sang, laughed, prayed the Rosary and solved many of the world's problems—all except our own. All the cathedrals mentioned above were dedicated to Mary, the Mother of God!

# Bernadette Leads The Way

Over the years, I have visited the Shrine of the Blessed Mother in Lourdes, France, nine times. My strong attachment to Our Lady of Lourdes began back in my first assignment at Maryville Academy in Des Plaines. On arriving in June 1944, I saw an exact replica of the Lourdes Shrine on the front lawn, built in thanksgiving to Mary for shielding the 850 children from the polio scourge. Father Eugene Mulcahey, the director of the school, had promised this to Mary.

In the ensuing years, in my walks between the rectory and the boys' yard, I found myself looking at the shrine four and five times a day. I saw, especially, young Bernadette, kneeling in the Grotto with her eyes fixed intently on Mary. Her beauty had captured Bernadette's heart.

In season and out of season, in snow and cold, in rains, in heat of summer, the child Bernadette, about 13 years old, kept her faithful vigil of prayer to Our Lady of the Immaculate Conception on our front lawn at Maryville. I came to see in the young girl the symbol of steadfastness and faithfulness to prayer. I would say to myself, often in those years, "In all the happenings of life, Bernadette held on to her desire to pray. Not even the police in Lourdes could scare her away from the Grotto of Massabielle, where Mary beckoned her to come for prayer."

In my own inner life at Maryville, I tried to imitate Bernadette by being faithful to prayer at the Grotto several times a day. The whole story of the appearances of Mary to the child took on a special fascination for me, inspiring me to make myself worthy of Mary's love. At the end of long days, I would bring myself, sometimes half-asleep, into the school chapel to spend time in sharing the day's happenings with the Lord and His Mother, Our Lady of Lourdes. Friendship with Bernadette brought me often to France and Lourdes. Bernadette's affliction of bronchial trouble did not leave after her 18 visits with Mary at the Grotto, next to the River Gave. Mary told her, "I do not promise you happiness here on Earth, but happiness in Heaven." The young visionary was to enter a convent, close by Lourdes, and eventually die at an early age of 33, after much suffering through the years. Never did she put away her spirit of prayer or complain about her poor lot in life.

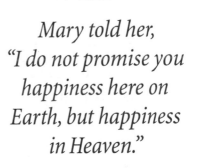

*Mary told her, "I do not promise you happiness here on Earth, but happiness in Heaven."*

We can learn much from Bernadette's story to stay faithful to union with Mary in prayer, no matter what our life's circumstances are.

# The Mystery Of Suffering

Through the years, I came to know an American Franciscan Religious, Brother Francis, assigned to work in the Holy Sepulcher Church in the Old City of Jerusalem. Oftentimes, he helped me vest for Mass on Mt. Calvary and in the Tomb of Christ, both of which are under the roof of Holy Sepulcher Church, the most revered shrine in the Holy Land.

One clear day, in a recent year, while visiting on Mt. Thabor, the Mount of the Transfiguration of Christ in Galilee, I suddenly came face to face with Brother Francis. Surprised to see him in this high place, 2000 feet above the plains below and 70 miles from his usual assignment in Jerusalem, I asked him why he had come to Mt. Thabor.

His story told of a defenseless man being attacked by robbers in Holy Sepulcher Church. The vandals flung Brother Francis down a long flight of stairs, breaking many of his bones and causing painful injuries. Here on Mt. Thabor, he was beginning a long period of recuperation from this vicious experience with his usual spirit of cheerfulness and good will.

How natural for one to complain to Christ, "Lord,

why didn't you take better care of me in the holiest shrine in Jerusalem?" But Brother Francis had not entered religious life to escape suffering! In no way did he need perfect protection from hardships to believe in the Lord's love for him.

At that time, as I walked about on this sacred mountain, I thought of the glorious vision of the Transfigured Christ that the Apostles, Peter, James and John had enjoyed in this moun- tain retreat. For a few moments, these bewildered disciples had tasted the ecstasy of Heaven to prepare them for the dark days of persecution ahead.

In the course of life, hardships, injuries, painful accidents, heart-breaking disappointments come to the people of God. These happen, despite long years of loving service and faithfulness to Christ. Taking these misfortunes in stride, with no bitterness in their hearts, these hurting people go on in the spirit of Brother Francis mentioned above.

*The vandals flung Brother Francis down a long flight of stairs, breaking many of his bones and causing painful injuries.*

One poem took the word, "disappointments," removed the letter "d" and inserted the letter "H." "Disappointments" became "His appointments."

I took my meeting with Brother Francis on Mt. Thabor as a message from God. As it were, Christ was revealing Himself to me in a glorious vision. Since then, I went through a series of trying, difficult experiences where I needed all the courage that I could muster from this vision to survive as a priest. I did survive!

*Father McKenna offering the Mass at the Tomb of Christ, Holy Sepulcher Church.*

# Signs On The Road Of Life

A lbuquerque, New Mexico, Thursday, October 20, 1994. Truly named the Land of Enchantment, this State provides sheer delight to the eyes of a visitor: the serpentine Rio Grande River, mountains, long vistas of unparalleled beauty in the rolling plains and colors no words can describe. Today, with two friends, one who lives in this city on a bluff overlooking the Rio Grande, I plan to drive north to the Marian Shrine of Chimayo, called the Lourdes of New Mexico.

During the day, as never before, I am impressed with the importance of road signs. With my local friend driving, we come upon many helpful markers on our trip north: Los Alamos (the birthplace of the A-Bomb), Las Cruces, Santa Fe. Because of these directional signs, we turn with confidence at all the major junctions, knowing that we are on the right road.

All of us desire happiness, even in this life on Earth. Everything we do, even our sins, is directed to bringing happiness to ourselves. God, in His Love for us, has given us signs on the road of life to lead us to this earthly destination of happiness, peace and self-fulfillment. These are the Ten Commandments, positive markers which will point the way to the greatest measure of true happiness possible on this Earth.

Returning from Chimayo, where we left our requests for help with Mary, we come to a highway junction without signposts. For the first time today, forced to guess, we make the wrong turn and lose an hour going in the wrong direction. Some people look on the Ten Commandments as shackles and handcuffs which take away our liberty and freedom. With disregard for these road signs, they wander into many unhappy situations, never arriving at their desired destination: lasting peace of soul in this life. They lose their way, sometimes forever.

One day a beggar asked Jesus for the gift of sight. "Lord, I want to see." Of course, the Lord granted his request. Daily, our prayer could be the same. "Jesus, we wish to see." We need spiritual sight to notice these most welcome signposts God provides for us on our journey to Heaven. As we drive along through the silence of the darkening, mountain highways, I keep thinking of this one idea. Keep alert and watchful for the road signs God gives us.

> *One day a beggar asked Jesus for the gift of sight. "Lord, I want to see."*

Mistakenly, many see the Ten Commandments as

"Thou Shalt Nots"—negative statements. How positive they are. Reverence the one true God. Respect God's Holy Name. Keep holy the day devoted to God. Respect one's Mother and Father. Have love for others. Revere one's own sexuality and the sexuality of others. Respect the property of others. Be truthful. Your neighbor's wife and possessions are precious. Respect them.

# Guideposts To Happiness

1    Adore Only Me, The One True God!

2    Revere My Name!

3    Worship Me On The Sabbath!

4    Respect Your Mother And Father!

5    Have Respect (Love) For Yourself And Others!

6    Respect Your Own Gift Of Sexuality And The Gift Of Sexuality In Others!

7    Be Honest!

8    Be Truthful!

9    Respect Your Neighbor's Wife!

10   Respect Your Neighbor's Goods!

# About the Author

Father McKenna, the youngest son of Irish immigrants, spent the first 25 years of his priesthood as a teacher—first at Maryville Academy, then at Quigley Seminary. At Quigley, he was the spiritual director, guiding young high school students in learning ways of righteousness and prayer. During the second half of his career, Father served as pastor and associate pastor at several parishes on the southwest side of Chicago. He also spent some time as a missionary in the Fairbanks (Alaska) diocese.

As Father neared retirement, he took on the challenge of establishing a chapel at Chicago's Midway Airport, which was experiencing a rebirth. Although technically retired, Father has now moved into his third career, ministering to air travelers and airport employees.

A lifelong resident of Chicago, Illinois, Father McKenna has been a world traveler, seeking inspiration across the globe. He has made twenty pilgrimages to Jerusalem. Father's favorite places to visit and write about are the Holy Land and Paris, France.

For fun, Father enjoys playing a good game of golf, especially with many of his fellow 290 retired priests in the Chicago area. He is the eight-time Senior Golf Champion of the Retired Priests of Chicago Association, having won their annual tournament each year (except one) he entered the competition.

On March 5, 1999, Father McKenna received the Archbishop James E. Quigley Distinguished Alumnus Award for special recognition and outstanding lifetime achievements.

After more than 55 years in the priesthood, Father continues to fulfill his life's mission of encouraging people everywhere to love God and others. You may contact the author by writing him at the address below; he would love to hear from you.

**Father George McKenna**
9720 S. Kedzie Avenue
Evergreen Park, IL 60805-3316

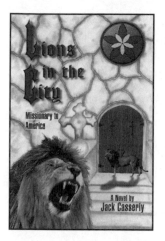

## LIONS IN THE CITY

Missionary to America

A Novel by Jack Casserly

Deluxe Softbound Edition © 2000

French fold-out covers

191 pages

6 x 9

$19.95 plus Shipping & Handling

Father Martin Mulloy, an American missionary, after laboring for 32 years in the African bush (Ghana), returns home to the U.S. in 1998 expecting to die from malaria. Instead, he lives, encountering the two greatest challenges of his life: the controversial changes in the Catholic Church following the Ecumenical Council of Vatican II and a soul-wrenching, face-to-face confrontation with his older brother, a fellow priest.

Penned by best-selling author, Jack Casserly, *Lions in the City* is a down-to-earth story of humanity, humility, and hope. His novel reveals today's conflicts between Catholic traditionalists and futurists, not with hair-splitting theological terms, but through all-too-human riveting drama. The narrative discloses the inside – often hidden – strife among Catholic leaders and its tragic result: fallen-away faithful in the hundreds of thousands.

---

"As one who spent 15 years in the Philippines, I fell in love with Father Martin and his simplicity…All in all, this is quite a book! Not only an enjoyable story, but one to challenge the reader."

—Rev. George P. Carlin, Foreign Missionary and Former Journalist

"It's all here…clerical bureaucracy, sexual freedom and its consequences, rectory loneliness, the temptations of drug and alcohol…the quest for meaning of existence which has characterized mankind for generations."

—Barrett McGurn, Retired Vatican Correspondent

*The* **I'LL ONLY SPEAK FOR 3 MINUTES** *Book Series*
By Father George McKenna

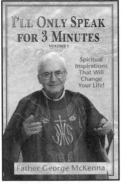

## VOLUME 1

© 1998
Trade pb, 99 pages
$10.95 plus S & H
The first volume contains an uplifting collection of thirty-seven brief, easy-to-read homilies from the founder of Chicago's Midway Airport Chapel. These warmhearted messages are for people of all ages, walks of life, and faiths.

## VOLUME 2

© 1999
Trade pb, 102 pages
$10.95 plus S & H
Father McKenna shares three dozen more of his famous three-minute sermons in this second collection. His engaging stories and practical insights offer simple and creative approaches to making a profound difference in your life.

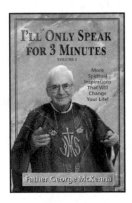

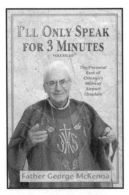

## VOLUME 3

© 2000
Trade pb, 101 pages
$10.95 plus S & H
Volume three offers the reader another collection of thirty-seven new, three-minute homilies by a master storyteller. These are Father's favorite parables, special ones that give comfort, offer guidance, and provide inspiration to all.

# Three-Minute Trilogy

Order all three volumes of Father McKenna's uplifting books on spiritual advice. You will treasure his 110 timeless literary gems for years to come. $30.00 plus S & H.

---

## Free Gifts!

Order any three Spiritual Inspiration titles from VCA Publishing and receive a copy of *The Secret of the Rosary* by St. Luis De Monfort, as well as a rosary personally blessed by Father George McKenna. (A $5.50 value!)

---

## Our Lady of Loreto Chapel

**Live in the Chicago Area?**
**Visiting the Windy City?**

Mass is offered at the Chicago Midway Airport Chapel on the weekends in the "B" Concourse. Signs are posted and announcements made prior to services.

SATURDAY — 3:45 pm
SUNDAY — 8:30 am

Mass lasts one-half hour † Confessions heard upon request † Communion is available before and after the Mass † Hear one of Father McKenna's famous three-minute homilies in person † Take home a complimentary bulletin † Pick up FREE blessed rosaries (by Father McKenna), traveler prayer cards, Care Notes™, and Catholic literature † Purchase autographed copies of Father's books from the Chapel Volunteer Workers or have him personalize ones you have already bought † Come as you are † Everyone is welcome! † Please call Airport Information (**1-773-838-0600** ) for any last-minute schedule or gate changes

## THE WHOLE PARENT: BOOK ONE

*12 Steps to Serenity for Unwed Parents*
By Margot Sheahan
Trade pb, 5-1/2 x 8-1/2
$12.95 plus S & H
Available: WINTER 2001

Margot Sheahan, the founder of *Unwed Parents Anonymous, Inc.,* has written a life guide for helping families deal with the problems of out-of-wedlock parenting. Her twelve-step program suggests change for these persons, a chance to feel serene, happy, and in control of their lives. This book will teach them acceptance of their situation, along with a forgiving, non-judgmental attitude toward others. Her practical guide cannot provide all the answers to their problems—no single book can—but it does offer a promise of understanding and the hope of serenity by following its precepts.

---

## CATHOLIC PROPHECIES FOR THE NEW MILLENNIUM

Astrological Interpretations
Of Saintly Predictions
Commentary by James E. Higgins III
(aka Nischintya Dasa)
Trade pb, 5-1/2 x 8-1/2
$10.95 plus S & H
Available: SPRING/SUMMER 2001

Famous Vedic astrologer and spiritual advisor James E. Higgins (aka Nischintya Dasa) examines the prophecies and predictions of Catholic saints, the Bible, and apparitions of the Blessed Mother. He claims, as we start the new millennium, that the Apocalypse is upon us. The Last Judgment, foretold by the prophets, martyrs, and mystics since antiquity, will come to pass – unless we get down on our knees and pray! Is it the end of civilization as we know it? Provocative, shocking, ominous.

# Also Available from VCA Publishing

## Healing Others: A Practical Guide — Walter Weston

5x8 trade paper, 176 pages     $11.95
Hampton Roads Publishing Company

The art of healing others through therapeutic prayer is not a skill limited to only a few people. It can be learned. Not simply theory or conjecture, this practical guide presents everything one needs to begin healing others, as told by a healer with more that 20 years extensive experience. Book one in a three-volume series.

## Healing Yourself: A Practical Guide — Walter Weston

5x8 trade paper, 176 pages     $11.95
Hampton Roads Publishing Company

*Healing Yourself: A Practical Guide* is the second of three volumes dealing with the theory and practice of healing. The same principles introduced in *Healing Others* can be applied to healing oneself. Here Weston provides everything one needs to begin self-healing through prayer. Book two in a three-volume series.

## How Prayer Heals: A Scientific Approach — Walter Weston

5x8 trade paper, 256 pages     $12.95
Hampton Roads Publishing Company

*How Prayer Heals*, the third of three volumes dealing with the theory and practice of healing, presents the science behind the art of healing through therapeutic prayer. People have been healing themselves and others for untold generations, but only recently has science discovered why therapeutic prayer works. Weston has over 20 years of extensive experience using prayer as an effective healing tool. *How Prayer Heals* is an insightful and revealing guide to the dynamics of faith and prayer. Book three in a three-volume series.

**Three Volume Set** (Regularly $36.85)     **$35**

# Order Form

Name _____

Address _____

City _____ State _____ Zip _____

| Quantity | Description | Product Code | Price | Subtotal |
|---|---|---|---|---|
| | I'll Only Speak for 3 Minutes, Vol. 1 | MCK1 | $10.95 | |
| | I'll Only Speak for 3 Minutes, Vol. 2 | MCK2 | $10.95 | |
| | I'll Only Speak for 3 Minutes, Vol. 3 | MCK3 | $10.95 | |
| | Three-Minute Trilogy (3-Vol. Set) | MCKT | $30.00 | |
| | Lions in the City | LION | $19.95 | |
| | Healing Others | WW1 | $11.95 | |
| | Healing Yourself | WW2 | $11.95 | |
| | How Prayer Heals | WW3 | $12.95 | |
| | 3-Volume Healing Set | WW4 | $35.00 | |

| Shipping Chart | |
|---|---|
| **Please add $1.00 for each of these items:**<br>MCK1, MCK2, MCK3, WW1, WW2, WW3<br>**Please add $2.00 for each of these items:**<br>MCKT, WW4, LION<br><br>Maximum of $7.00 for shipping charges | Merchandise Subtotal |
| | Shipping Charges (see chart at left) (Maximum $7.00) |
| All U.S. orders are shipped via Priority Mail, usually within 24 hours | Handling Charge — $3.00 |
| Order any three Spiritual Inspiration titles: receive a free book and rosary! | Illinois residents add 8.75% Sales Tax |
| | **TOTAL ORDER** |

Please send check or money order to:
**VCA Publishing • P.O. Box 388352 • Chicago, IL 60638-8352**

**Credit Card customers may order by visiting our website or calling our toll-free number:**
**www.govedic.com**